SINGLE IN AMERICA

Before Texting & Tinder

True stories from 1989. Still true today.

By David M. Kleinman and Danna M. Kelley

About the Authors (AKA "The Two DMKs")

David M. Kleinman was married once upon a time and wants to try it again some day. He lives in the New York metro area.

Danna Marie Kelley has raised one darling son and several mischievous animals. She is single and lives in Charlottesville, Virginia.

Contents

VII. Impersonal Ads   163

"Promise, large promise, is the soul of an advertisement."
Samuel Johnson

Preface

The heart is a lonely hunter. Carson McCullers
The more things change, the more they stay the same. French proverb

What you hold in your hands first came into being 26 years ago as a collection of stories based on interviews we conducted with a wide range of single men and women, young and old, from many walks of life. A few were prominent in their fields; most were obscure — it didn't matter.

Our method in 1989 was to mix journalism with narrative storytelling. Before Reality TV, we started "filming" life as we found it. Sampling from across the anthropological dig of the singles landscape, we allowed the subjects to speak in their own voices, and joined their oral histories thematically to create a novelistic shape. Then we curated this colorful anthology of cuddly and not-so-cuddly males and females in the endless permutations of mating (and un-mating) as a modern *Canterbury Tales*.

Our stories portray individuals who each respond in their own way to the particular challenges of the heart and mind faced by singles. Some folks led us to others and were related in some way, giving us the chance to intertwine their stories. We think that makes things more interesting for the reader as well. We used real names when we were given permission, and made up the names when permission was granted for use of the story but not the name.

Our book was compelling enough back then to be optioned by a Hollywood producer (Crane Wexelblatt Entertainment) as the basis for a TV show that was seriously considered by then CBS president Jeff Sagansky and almost "put into production" by NBC. Another *almost* was Fredrica Friedman, associate publisher of Little, Brown at the time, who was enthusiastic about the book but balked at the sizable advance our literary agent demanded. When neither book nor TV show came to pass, we, the authors, put the project on ice and went our separate ways.

Now, 26 years later, we've reunited as authors, slimmed the work down to the most representative stories, and focused solely on the characters who best stand the test of time.

The year 1989, when we compiled this work, was a landmark year in pop culture: *Seinfeld* (the quintessential "Single in NYC" show) debuts, and Taylor Swift is born (her 2014 hit album is titled: *1989*). Even more so in the larger world: Berlin Wall falls. Soviet Union collapses. Oliver North convicted in Iran-Contra scandal. Tiananmen Square massacres. Fatwa against Salman Rushdie for *The Satanic Verses*. US troops invade Panama, Noriega captured. P.W. Botha quits as South Africa's president. Exxon Valdez oil spill in Alaska. *Born on the Fourth of July* opens, and *Rainman* wins the Oscar. That's already a lot, and there's a lot more.

Big data was not yet an everyday term. Living your life online had no meaning. There were no smartphones, no Internet, no tablets, no apps, no Twitter, no Facebook, no LinkedIn, no Cloud — their impact on the mating game, well, that's a story for another day — yet our 1989 single folks are people we recognize today.

While set a quarter century ago, we can still relate to these men and women locked inside this time capsule. Which is why we're setting them free. Readers should note that in 1989 our world was narrower, not as diverse and inclusive as it thankfully is today, and our stories reflect that. Our hope is that whatever your ethnicity, sexual orientation, or skin color, our characters' wholly human stories will resonate with you.

We have included brief epilogues whenever possible to answer the natural question: What ever happened to them? Where are they today?

Inquiring minds wanna know.

David M. Kleinman and Danna M. Kelley
August 2015

I. THE RUGGED INDIVIDUALIST

"Let a man accept his destiny, no pity and no tears."
Euripides

End of the Trail

A Great Blue Heron circles above the two-lane highway to Paul Smiths, a Mormon college town at the northwestern edge of the Adirondack Park. As the bird rides the updraft, the wacky call of an Adirondack loon is heard on Saranac Lake's lower Chautauqua, thirty miles from Keene. Narrow views of the lake peep through at intervals along the road, glimmers of light through the shadowy trees.

Stands of white and yellow birch and pine, hemlocks, balsams and evergreens line the blacktopped highway to the Adirondack Visitors Interpretive Center, affectionately known as "the VIC." Folks who make it as far as the parking lot reach an enclave in the trees where the silence is felt.

By seven P.M., the center's three-story atrium of wood beams and glass is filled with sweet-voiced grandparents accompanying their children and grandchildren to a social event uniquely Adirondack. It's a coffee klatch for the ecology-minded. As show time approaches, their reverential mood deepens.

Anne LaBastille, "tonight's illustrious speaker," as she is soon to be introduced, is a single woman in her fifties, a self-made legend in these parts, an Adirondack Park Commissioner, a scientist and woodswoman. In the late seventies, she wrote a book called *Woodswoman*, fusing ecology, self-reliance and her quest to find a personal place in nature.

The freeze-up on Black Bear Lake is a prelude to winter. The freeze-up is a prelude to hardship. The freeze-up is a prelude to loneliness. It begins on a November evening as a filigreed fingering of ice along the shoreline. The freeze-up is an event as important in nature as the solstices, equinoxes, full moon and eclipses. It affects the living patterns of many fish and wildlife species. And it dramatically changes my lifestyle on this Adirondack lake where I live alone in the log cabin I built myself.

While Anne is more comfortable talking about the environment than her personal life, in her books she says plenty about her marriage, her divorce, and two subsequent love affairs that ended when she decided that marriage would compromise her independence, and she and her partners simply went their separate ways.

Her subject at the VIC this cool July evening is not romance. It's the Guatemalan grebe, a bird she tried for 24 years to save from extinction. She's worried about the politics of environmental problems, not where she's going to get a date tonight.

Acid rain, acidified lakes, devastated trees in the Adirondacks are symptoms in one endangered wilderness. What about the rainforests of the Amazon and Borneo? What about ozone depletion and global warming? What about our polluted oceans and seas? What we want to know, however, is what about Anne? Is one person's life too insignificant in comparison?

Fanning out in all directions are the VIC's three thousand acres of protected habitat. Behind one of the center's three main buildings, Anne arrives in her red pickup truck. Bumper stickers read, "Conserve Water & Soil" and "Plant Trees." It has a camper top and canoe attached to its flat-bed from which spring Anne's constant companions, Condor and Chekika, her German shepherds.

Dignified and self-possessed, Anne is dressed in sandals, white slacks and a flowing green blouse. From her neck hangs a likeness of the giant grebe, carved by a Guatemalan artisan. Anne is amiable, has a pleasing smile, but beneath the casual byplay, she's all business.

"I don't like to gossip," she tells a magazine reporter, vainly trying to probe something other than "the big issues." She is five foot four, surprisingly tiny, with long, blonde braids to either side of her Germanic face. She is frequently described as "petite, pretty, feminine." The adjectives are used ironically, as if impossible to square with the persona of the woodswoman: rugged, independent, wielding a chain saw and swinging an axe. A surprising touch is Anne's light gloss of pale pink lipstick.

In the VIC's atrium, much of the muffled chatter is about the woodswoman who remains something of an enigma. She is not universally loved — one critic called her "condo woman" after she spent a few winters in considerably less rustic surroundings than her cabin on Black Bear Lake. All the same, she's written four books, has her Ph.D. in wildlife ecology from Cornell and in 1988 was named Conservationist of the Year by the Audubon Society.

Whether they like her or not, or even know her or not, everyone waiting for her talk has an opinion.

"She's an amazing woman! But watch out if you don't suit her purposes. She can be rather unfriendly."

"She's an extraordinary gal — pretty and knows how to handle an axe!"

"LaBastille in French, doesn't that mean prison? She's guarded, to say the least."

* * *

Many greet news of Anne LaBastille's singularly single life with bemusement. How could anyone, in 1989, live alone, among bears and barred owls, in an unheated cabin in the wilderness? New Agers may opt for country homes with amenities, a refuge from their professional city lives, but this is too rugged. Too extreme. Can she really live alone in the woods with her dogs and her trees successfully substituting for a "significant other"? However dedicated she is to her calling, is it enough? Isn't something missing?

Early that winter, Anne welcomed us to her cabin, reached after a long hike from the nearest road and a boat ride across Black Bear Lake. Seeing her in these surroundings, it's impossible to imagine her living in a city walkup somewhere. With Chekika and Condor ever-present, Anne prepares a tasty meal of roast chicken, potatoes and honeyed squash. A kettle boils atop her cast-iron stove. Navajo rugs, blankets and Guatemalan Indian curtains add a touch of colorful hominess, with bookshelves and a cluttered desk showing signs of Anne's busy work life. Deer antlers serve as racks for guns, fishing rods and clothing.

Her porch, where she often chooses to type, sports several rockers and a Brazilian hammock. Her log studio is graced by broad views of her isolated lake.

Environmentalism for Anne is not a picket line but her own 23-acre backyard where she has developed personal relation-ships not with men but with trees. It sounds kooky, but she wrote about it in *Woodswoman* without a trace of self-consciousness.

"The first trees I got to know, and later draw strength from were the mature, towering red spruces and white pines.

"As I became more tuned into trees, I began to admire the enormous white pine near the path to the outhouse. I even oriented the entrance of the outhouse so that I could gaze at this tall, furrowed tree while sitting there. It was much better than reading Time *magazine.*

"In getting to know my trees, an exceptional event occurred. On my trips back and forth to the outhouse, I took more and more enjoyment from touching the great white pine. One morning, with my arms wrapped around the trunk, I began to feel a sense of well-being. I held on for over fifteen minutes, chasing extraneous thoughts from my mind. The rough bark was pressed hard against my skin. It was as though the tree was pouring its life-force into my body."

* * *

Anne is wearing a wool sweater, dungarees and sneakers. This morning she finished the first draft of her book about the giant grebes of Guatemala; the entire first draft has been completed in three months, and she's clearly elated.

"When I write, my muse is with me, takes over completely. How could I have that with a husband and child?" she asks. "I wouldn't have the creative solitude I need. How could I write a book in three months?"

Coming to the Adirondacks for the first time as a teenager with a summer job at a small resort, she instantly knew this was where she wanted to be. She was "simultaneously smitten" with love for her boss. She was twenty; he was forty when they married. Her married years were hectic, an indentured servitude to the resort's guests. After seven years, she found her way out of her domestic wilderness, and doesn't seem likely to turn back. "The single format works best for me now," Anne says. "I don't care for the notion that loneliness goes with singleness because I've been married and I was just as alone married with a man who didn't appreciate me and wasn't sensitive to my needs, to the little fragile bird that's in my soul that was struggling to get out and be somebody in life.

"At times I was so desperately lonely in my marriage and there didn't seem to be any hope of getting out of it, and that can be more frightening than being single, being free, being lonely but knowing that at any time you cared to make a move you can end the loneliness."

Anne doesn't seem particularly lonely in her woods. "Everyone gets lonely. It's the human condition," says Anne, the social scientist, the single woman living alone. "The whole problem with American life is we're brainwashed to think we should always be happy, we should always be fulfilled, we should always have a beautiful partner, we should always have all these wonderful, good things, but life isn't that way. When you don't have those expectations, it's easier."

The quiet on Black Bear Lake seems impenetrable. Here, getting a date, or finding a mate, are remote concerns. "If there's anything I can do with the years I have left, I want to alarm the human population to try and save the natural world, because we can't live without it and it's going so fast."

Having a creative muse may be fortifying, but what's it like at the end of the day when the muse goes home for the night? Surely even the muse takes time off.

"It's a lot less lonely in the wilderness than coming home after work in the city and going to an apartment alone and being afraid to walk out at night 'cause some guy'll mug you, or not having any place to go except a bar or a movie. The options are so limited in a city," says Anne.

If she feels lonely in the woods, there's always a ready antidote. "I find I'm so in tune with nature that if I go out in the woods and I hear the red squirrels in the trees, or maybe I see a deer leaping off through the forest, or I go down by the lake and a beaver goes by, or I come up into a swamp and I hear the peepers or a frog, I immediately feel better," she says.

A Woodsman for the Woodswoman would be nice, but he'd have to be a real soulmate, someone on her wavelength, sharing her concerns and her style of life, and she doesn't dwell on it. "I don't obsess about it," says Anne, "it's not worthwhile. Let's face it, I live a mile and a half from a road, I'm not exactly sitting in a hot pickup spot."

Loneliness may be inevitable, but to Anne it comes in three varieties. Loneliness that can be divided this way may not be so overwhelming. Scientist that she is, her effort is to understand. It's the principle of "Know thy enemy."

"One kind of loneliness is the twilight loneliness at the end of a day when I've been writing, and it's all drained out of me," she says. "I've chopped my wood, I've played with the dogs. Around twilight, I start feeling, well, it would be nice if there was someone to talk to, a companion, someone to joke with, and that's a lonely time. For one thing, your blood sugar's at a low, your energy's at a low, you haven't had dinner, you're kind of shifting gears."

"The second kind of loneliness you don't feel very often," she says. "There's a wonderful German word called *veltschmertz*, it means world pain. Only Germans would have a word like that. It's a feeling you get sometimes after a holiday, sometimes on a Sunday afternoon like right about now, when you'll be sitting all by yourself and no one has called, nobody has written, no mail that day, and you feel really out of touch.

"I start thinking about all the poor people that are in nursing homes, like my mom was for seven years, and all the poor people who are being tortured in some damn prison in some underdeveloped country somewhere, and all the terrible states of being alive that exist on this planet, and I get this pain, this lonely, sad pain about what is the human condition and what can I do about it. And there's nothing I can do about it. That's part of the pain; it's just sort of a general malaise for the sadness of humanity.

"The third kind is a different kind of lonesome; my little tiny chunk of protoplasm up against this big force of nature. I don't know what that big force is going to do and it doesn't care, you know, it's totally implacable. I'm nothing in terms of the big picture and that's a real lonesome feeling. When you live close to nature, nature rules. And I tell you, lots of terrible things could happen and I feel real lonesome then."

Loneliness is no bugbear; in fact, Anne fears not being alone enough. These days, her urge for solitude is stronger than any propelling toward someone else. "I would worry if I let somebody into my life, into my circle. If we decided to live together at my cabin, I would say, Whoa, am I gonna get enough personal space, enough private time? Is that person going to understand that I need good chunks of aloneness, whether it's to think or to write or to contemplate, or whatever it is that I'm doing? That would be one of my major worries."

Anne serves us dinner and politely answers our questions. Playing with her dogs as we talk, it's as if she can't quite figure out what we're driving at. She likes to talk about the big issues, and all we want to know is "Where are the guys?"

Lecturing twelve times a year, appearing before large audiences of "my kind of people, the Audubon Society, biology departments at colleges," you'd think she'd meet the right sort of man. She concedes that, presented with a lecture hall filled with men, she can't help wondering what they're like. But so far nothing's come of it.

"I think it's pretty safe to say I never ever met a man at one of those lectures who's come up and just seemed to be a soulmate, someone who could understand where I was coming from and could share life. They're either in the fan or groupie category, or they're kooky birds, or they're married, or too old, or too young, it's very odd.

"I've talked to my girlfriends about that, and they say I probably threaten a lot of men because I get up there and I talk about chopping wood and going to the Amazon. They must wonder, is this an Amazon herself? Who wants to get next to her? It's kinda scary."

Chekika whines, and Anne gives the dog's red bandana a gentle, reprimanding tug. "No, baby, we're going to take your ball away if you don't lie down and be quiet."

Anne says that when she wrote her book about wilderness women, "I met a lot of women who are very independent and work outdoors which makes you more independent. By contrast, I know a lot of women who are convinced that the only way they can have a happy life is to have a partner. That's ridiculous. I know women who won't learn to pick up an axe and chop wood. At my cabin it says 'LaBastille, you can handle anything.'"

"You can handle anything," says Anne. "That's what you've got to believe in life to succeed and it doesn't have anything to do with being single or being married or having a partner or anything. It means having confidence in yourself to just do what it takes to get through and to endure. I just wish that more women would have that point of view, that you can handle anything. And having a man around doesn't make it any different."

Anne may not be single by choice. Maybe she would have liked one of her romantic liaisons to have worked out. But she's no victim of singlehood.

"I'm not out hunting for a man... because I'm more interested in the other things. I guess that's a way of being single."

Epilogue

"Anne LaBastille, best known as the author of the four-volume 'Woodswoman' autobiography, died on July 1, 2011, at a nursing home in Plattsburgh, N.Y. She was 75. Her death was confirmed by the Adirondack Park Agency, for which she had served as a commissioner from 1975 to 1993." From* The New York Times *19-paragraph obituary on July 11.*

Despite her heroic, often solitary efforts to save the Guatemalan grebe, the last of the birds was seen in 1989, the same year as our interview with Anne. The grebe was officially declared extinct.

She Paddles Her Own Canoe

While vacationing in the Adirondacks, Mike Sands drove to the Visitors Interpretive Center to hear Anne LaBastille's lecture on the Guatemalan grebe. In the back of his mind, he'd hoped to meet someone, a young, unattached mountain woman perhaps. In the atrium that evening, he did meet an unattached mountain woman.

Standing a few feet away was Gertrude Thompson. As bright eyed as a four-year old, with the energy of a toddler in a playpen, the eighty-two-year old leans cockily on her cane, observing the world like an eagle from its aerie.

"This atrium stuff is all right angles, too confining," she says, to no one in particular. "Too many horizontal beams." She has high cheekbones, wears no makeup, and her eyes have a mischievous glint in them.

"I don't know," Mike says, attracted to her vitality. "It's open and airy. Not bad as far as atriums go."

"It ain't nothin," she shoots back. "There are no right angles in nature." She almost sounds angry. "Buckminster Fuller taught me that in '33 when he was still foolin' around with his three-wheeled automobile." Already you're getting the picture, this is someone with interests.

She says her husband, Lin Thompson, worked with Buckminster Fuller. "Bucky invented the geodesic dome. My husband designed the 38-foot eagles on the Greater Pittsburgh Airport. Our faces, you don't see any right angles there, do ya?"

Conspicuous in any crowd, Gertrude is a bohemian. She wears a white sailor's cap at a jaunty angle, a red pullover sweater that reaches below her waist, white slacks and sandals. Her aluminum cane is not a crutch so much as a sportily wielded appendage. The sailor's cap is pushed back far enough on her large head to reveal shiny grey pigtails tied across the top. "I live in a tent two feet longer than Anne LaBastille's," she declares. "I have no family. I'm an oddity."

Gertrude introduces her friend Norma Green. "She owns the land, I'm a squatter," Gertrude chuckles. Her tent on Upper Saranac Lake is pitched on Norma Green's 200-acre estate not twenty yards from the water. Gertrude's husband died 23 years ago and she's lived on Saranac Lake, June to September, ever since. She never remarried.

"What for? I don't want the entanglement."

Nine months of the year she lives in Ridgewood, New Jersey. "Twenty-one minutes from Manhattan's theater district if it isn't rush hour. I can just see the top of the George Washington Bridge through my rhododendrons and oak trees."

"I'm glad you picked me up," Mike says, agreeing to pay a visit.

"Serendipity!" she cries. "I love it! Call me at noon tomorrow and I'll give you directions." Her voice crackles with enthusiasm. "We're gonna have fun!"

* * *

After Bullpoint and Weebeck ("big rock" in Indian), Mike spotted the wooden sign leading to Gertrude's campsite. The letters, burned into the wood, read "Captain G.S. Thompson." He'd parked where she directed and made his way down the steps through the heavy growth of ferns and balsams, to her semi-cleared campsite.

The tent stands alongside a smallish boulder, "a pebble of anorthosite," Gertrude calls it, "rolled here by the glacier ten to twelve thousand years ago." In front of the rock are three of the commonest trees in the Adirondacks, a white birch, yellow birch and a hemlock. "I call the rock Chekhov, and the three trees, one, two, three, are the three sisters."

Beyond Chekhov and the three sisters is the boat dock, where Gertrude is bobbing. "I'll take you to Chapel Island now," Gertrude commands, steadying herself with her cane as she maneuvers in her sixteen foot, aluminum hulled motorboat. She orders her visitor to wait on the dock until she undoes all but the last rope. "It's not everybody has a woman sea captain," she chortles as she balances in the beam.

She's a gutsy thing as she lays her cane on the aluminum bottom. After four broken hips, she can't afford another fall, but damned if that will stop her. Afraid of nothing, Gertrude slowly but gamely makes her way to the tie lines, hobbled but not defeated. The process of undoing the lashes is painful and tricky, but Gertrude insists on doing it herself. She places one hand on a short, metal dock pole and the other on the long, wooden post to which it is lashed. "This is my lean, this is my pull. Isn't it great?"

What's great is Gertrude's capacity to be delighted by the smallest things. If this is old age, what is youth? Crossing to the starboard side, gingerly steadying herself, she chuckles, "My doctor made me promise to wear this infernal life jacket."

An arresting image... Gertrude Thompson, balancing in the aluminum boat alone, doing the old soft shoe on Saranac Lake.

"A rig like this without the motor costs about $1,600," Gertrude declares. She lowers the six horsepower motor behind her. "I had a four horsepower engine, but it didn't have the punch. Any larger than six, I wouldn't be able to lift it." She gives the small outboard motor's pull cord a good swift yank. Motor purring at last, Gertrude pilots them slowly away from shore.

"You see that dock? I designed it. It's a table when you turn it upside down, those four lashing poles become the four legs," she laughs. "Pretty clever, eh?"

Mike watches her tent camp disappear as they get further away from shore, surrounded by the distant mountains. "It's your own little choices that make all the big differences, that change the whole course of your life," Gertrude says over the sound of the engine. "I just tilt the rudder a little this way and we're off on a whole other track."

* * *

Gertrude's great great uncle sired Sinclair Lewis. Her father, William Swift, son of the founder of the Swift meatpacking empire ("real robber barons") was a British General, "not from Churchill's section, boom, boom, boom, boom, but from the engineer's division in India and South Africa.

"I started with kind of a bizarre background. I was an only child, so I've never been afraid. I was born four hours after my family landed in Philadelphia in 1907. They expected me to be born on the ocean. My father had a fight with the Crown over black people. He was building roads and bridges for the gold mines in Johannesburg and he refused to use child labor. So he resigned his South African commission. The Crown put Lord Haley in there, and he invented apartheid with the Dutch. There wouldn't have been apartheid if my father hadn't quit."

Gertrude's husband, Linwood W. Thompson, was an architect, a sculptor who worked with I.M. Pei on the design of the World Trade Center in New York City. "I had a classical education, but Lin was more creative, he had a real taste for the warps and wiggles of life," she says, "and during our forty years of married life, we embarked on many adventures.

"In the forties and fifties, we had an apartment in Greenwich Village and we were always hosting different people, artists, avant-garde and high society types. I don't care, I enjoy people, I have to have variety."

After two miscarriages, Gertrude and Lin adopted four children, including two Russian war orphans. Only two of her four adopted children are alive today; one, a U.S. Army cook stationed in Texas, visits Gertrude once a year when Navy ships put in to New York Harbor. The other "sends Kiwi from you know where."

You begin to see what she means about those infernal right angles, they're too predictable; life is filled with wobbles and curves.

One of life's biggest curves was also the longest time coming. "Lin was dying of cancer for thirty years, diagnosed and undiagnosed. When he got sicker and sicker, we came here, to the Adirondacks, because my husband and I could not go to hotels any more. He had cancer of the face and people fainted, and maître d's would say, 'Please, not today.'

"Didn't bother me, but Lin wasn't that way. I always loved fishing and hiking and we got the tent when we decided we'd have to go away from civilization. We backpacked and canoe-carried the tent to Axton on the Raquette River. But I moved it here when he died twenty-three years ago.

"His doctor told me Lin only had a few weeks left. And so I went to the dining table where Lin was sitting, I put my head on the table like this, you see. 'Doctor says I'll only be able to talk to you for three weeks more.'

"Lin says, 'I know!'

"He grabbed my pigtails in the middle and he gave them a mighty yank and said, 'You're a good squaw, Gertrude, and you can paddle your own canoe! People love you. Go to it!'

"And I've lived by that ever since. We have to sometimes have the nerve to say, 'Go to it!' That's been my major criterion for choices, about learning new things, which gave me the gorgeous, gorgeous horizon of God's world... the skyscape and the silence of the Adirondacks... 'I will look unto the hills from whence cometh my strength.'

"I get the batteries recharged in the Adirondacks. I can hardly stand life without thinking I am a citizen of the universe which is a much bigger democracy than the United States. A democracy! Where plants, animals, insects, and humans live together in a self-regulating world. Isn't that fascinating?"

* * *

She was fifty-nine when Lin died. After forty years of marriage she was alone. Gertrude took the bull by the horns and embarked on a new life. She felt less like a widow than an explorer. Getting married again was never a possibility.

"Oh, heaven's no. What for? I've had lots of fun, I go out when I want to, with whom I want to, and I don't care. But I'm not interested in getting married and entangled.

"I never wanted to get married again because, if we go to heaven, I don't want to go and say this is my husband, to my husband. Not me! I liked him! I'd rather run into my husband the way I was. If there is a heaven! He taught me how to think, to live creatively instead of my mechanical Greece and Rome, no thinking, no creativity, no daring!"

Pulling her right out of right angles?

"You bet! He did!"

Right angles will always give way to wiggles and warps but, through it all, Gertrude's love for Lin remains. "Never dies! It's a noun again. When he was here, it was a verb."

God's gorgeous horizon is not just the lake, the mountains, the skyscape; it's also Gertrude's garden. Her twelve by four-teen foot tent (built up in places like a cabin) stands in a slight clearing in the woods. The grass around it is mowed once a week by Norma Green's caretaker. The campsite, surrounded by thick conifers and hardwoods, has a gentle knoll leading to the lake.

"You don't worry about ticks here?" asks the city boy who is half her age, three times her size.

"Nah! I don't worry about anything! There isn't time," she fires back, as she takes him on a two-penny tour of her tent, her most inventive contribution to God's gorgeous horizon on the lake. No space within the small, yet durable structure is wasted. Living is an exercise in inventiveness here. "The orange stuff is canvas, and then the fly is on top," Gertrude explains. "I call it my rag house. I just got new lines. I have to get a fly every two or three years."

Gertrude pauses on her porch, before stepping inside. "Do you see the hemlocks there? In Kentucky they're called the wedding bell trees because they shed their cones in June.

I planted that one. Now what was I doing? I'm gonna put up some tea and close the screen for bugs.

"This is a studio apartment New York-style. Everything is convertible. Every wall is a room." The inside of her tent smells of cedar, of which the floor boards, walls and joints are made. Her tent actually has walls. Made of canvas.

"You know what this is?" asks Gertrude, like Mister Wizard quizzing a student about the contents of a glass beaker. "It's a hutch!" She's as tickled with the layout of her New York studio as a celestial engineer with the interior of a lunar lander. "This pulls out," she says, completing her demonstration of the dining room assembly, "and grandmother's lamp I can hang here and pull the table out and we have room for four.

"Now this is where I put my bedroll! And this is the attic and I bring in that stepladder... I call it my silver stairs... and when it's real cold I bank the fire and sleep up there because hot air rises. Great, huh?"

No detail escapes her scrutiny. Master the details, she seems to say, and you master everything.

"This is my kitchen, not bad, huh? This is my icebox and little freezer, it's convertible, it's bottled gas or electric. This is an apartment stove, bottled gas, this is my cans and my containers... And I have both honey and our own Bullpoint syrup for my visitors. Oh, boy! I love it!

"And this is my cellar, Mike. Paper products, tools, odds and ends. Everything a cellar needs, in about one hundredth the space! This is an ecologically sensitive tent!"

It's a magical mystery tour led by Gertrude in Wonderland; or the Mad Hatter, serving up more stops along the way than the Radio City Music Hall organ. Not only is she not burdened or put upon by the everyday routines of daily life, she makes an adventure of something as mundane as a kitchen shelf. "Oh, I just love playing house!"

* * *

With her two master's degrees in psychology, she worked until her seventy-first birthday as a counselor for institutionalized juveniles. "They didn't let you work after seventy so I waited until I was seventy-one to retire.

"When I retired, I asked myself, what gives me the most pleasure in life... what makes me happiest... what makes me feel most alive?

"It was reading. I was taught to read by an Indian Sikh, I didn't like my Methodist tutor. I decided if I liked to read better than anything else, I better get a subject that's all mine."

The professors at the Atmospheric Sciences Center soon got to know the spunky lady from Saranac Lake who began showing up at their free lectures.

"Well, one day they just told me I could come to their graduate classes if I wanted to audit them. I got so interested in physics, I couldn't think of anything else!"

One of her special subjects at the research center was lightning. "It amazes me! Starts in the clouds at about 220,000 ohms but by the time it strikes the earth, it's ten times weaker. Why? Mono polar electricity, that's why!"

She studied chaos theory, learned of the butterfly effect ("a butterfly flapping its wings over Saranac Lake can change the weather two days later in Beijing!"), and indulged her endless appetite for learning everything from particle physics to the origin of the universe. She read to her heart's content. She had long conversations with her professors. She has a theory for everything. ("Ever meet anybody as long-winded as me?") Like the contents of her tent, her opinions could be catalogued from weather to ethics, astronomy to auto repair.

Mike and Gertrude sit on the screened porch of her "tent," munching buttered biscuits still warm from Gertrude's convection oven. Hummingbirds hover just outside the screen, attacking the sugar water solution Gertrude places in the cylindrical feeder.

"Look at us, sitting here!" she says. "We didn't know we'd meet. I was kidding Norma last night in the car as we drove back, 'that guy's coming to see me,' and she said, 'I kinda liked him in a quiet way, but I couldn't do that.'

"I said, 'Oh, don't be silly, it isn't the singles scene. We're not in a bar.' My friend Dr. Potter, she's an obstetrician, she says to me, 'Gertrude, your life is magic, do you know that? I say, 'Yes, I admit that. But I don't do anything, it just happens.'

"Lawrence Olivier was one of my favorites in the theater. You know what he said? 'The people who are unafraid and curious are the happiest.'"

* * *

It's late afternoon, the sun has dipped behind the mountains and, for Mike at least, it's a bit lonely as shadows lengthen. He gets lucky with one single woman during his trip to the Adirondacks, and she's eighty-two years old.

After enjoying Gertrude's last burst about non-Euclidean geometry ("You see, my face and shape don't fit this straight line, neither does a tree."), architecture ("Builders only used straight lines because they didn't know how to make their structures stay up!"), space ("Life is built on space. Between you and me. Between this and the tree, this and the stars... and the moon if you're courting."), and subatomic particles ("Everything's in flux, everything's made of the same basic stuff."), Mike bids Gertrude farewell.

"Maybe I'll see you in New York sometime," he says. Before leaving her all alone at her campsite, he asks her what she's doing tonight.

"I gotta read some more, ya know," Gertrude shoots back.

Epilogue

Death announcement published in The New York Times *on February 5, 1997:*

THOMPSON-Gertrude S. On February 3 in Ridgewood, NJ at age 89. The students, faculty and staff at the University at Albany, State University of New York, mourn the passing of Gertrude S. Thompson, a major benefactor dedicated to atmospheric science education and research at the University. She was an extraordinary woman with a love and commitment to the ecology of the Adirondack mountains. Generations of students will benefit from her philanthropy. Her legacy carries on.

II. EMMA'S FRIENDS

*"The human heart in conflict with itself...
only that is worth writing about."*
William Faulkner

Two Scorpios

Richie Adams thumps down the stairs of his SoHo loft at noon to get his mail. There it is, right on schedule: the annual birthday card from his crazy friend Nick the Wildman. Nick and he share the same birthday; they are both Scorpios and proud of it, living in the Age of Aquarius, born under the most sexual sign in the zodiac. Back in 1972, when they were students at the University of Kansas, the two of them shared a house with two or three other intense dreamers, out to save the world.

Other than their birthdays, they also share an insatiable appetite for analyzing, debating and theoretically solving the world's problems. Richie, the supreme strategist, master of the logical argument, the well-thought out position and beautifully turned phrase; Nick, the home-grown philosopher whose outrageous ideas sprang from something other than logic, had cosmic proportions, and more than a grain of truth. The two of them rarely agree on anything but their delight in disagreeing.

How differently their lives had turned out, Richie muses: he, dressing up in a suit every day to report to his "power position" at a Madison Avenue ad agency in New York City; Nick, still living the life of a Dharma Bum in Lawrence, Kansas.

Last May, during a business trip to Kansas City, Richie swung his rented Chrysler LeBaron west and paid a quick visit to his old friend.

* * *

Nick Wilder pulls a pair of faded jeans over his long, lean legs and tucks in a royal blue tee shirt emblazoned with the scarlet letters, "KU". KU stands for University of Kansas in Lawrence, Kansas where Nick has made his home for the past 20 years. On this May morning, the air is absolutely heady with the smells and sounds of spring. Nick's windows are flung open, sheer curtains billow into his sparsely furnished rooms on the ground floor of an old house in town.

He sits on the front porch swing, drinking a mug of coffee and watching students with early classes whiz by on bicycles, keeping an eye out for pretty girls wearing culottes. As he's lacing his work boots, a tow-headed boy bounds up the wooden steps, landing with a thud at Nick's side, "When are we going to work on the boat, Nick? Do you really think we can sail it to China?"

"Yeah, sure we can make it to China or we'll die trying. Either way it'll be an adventure, right? We'll talk about it later, champ. I gotta make tracks or I'll be late for work."

Nick swigs the last drop of coffee, feeds his two love birds, straps a well-worn tool belt around his waist and is off. Not having a car of his own, he walks to a buddy's house to catch a ride to work. They build houses. Nick's a carpenter who likes his work; he likes the toughness of it, the physicality of it; he appreciates good craftsmanship and can wax poetic over the symmetry of a well-built house.

At 38, Nick cuts an impressive figure striding through town.

He's 6' 4", lean and hard, broad shouldered and narrow hipped. His finely chiseled face bespeaks his Nordic heritage, and the red beard, once long and unkempt in the 70s, is now neatly trimmed. However, there's no mistaking it, he's a child of the 60s, an aging hippie who describes himself as a holdout.

This holdout who bemoans his bachelor status on one hand, revels in it on the other. For Nick, Lawrence, Kansas is a single man's paradise with an endless supply of nubile college girls for whom he never tires. Even if he can't touch, he can sure look. He's left Lawrence three times, but each time he's come back. He admits that at 18, he first came to Lawrence from Wichita "primarily for the women, and secondarily, if there was an education to be got, so be it." He feels about the same way at 38.

"I've had a lot of older women in this town in the past 20 years; I've had a lot of women, period. It never stops. I'll never get tired of beauty. Women my age are starting to look kind of old to me though. I'm more at ease now with students than I was at 18. As long as I don't end up toothless and bald, that's a fair thing to say. One phenomenon that I understand as a carpenter is that the older I get, the harder and meaner I get, but by the same token the more accepting, passive and compassionate I get.

"I'm not getting flabby or senile; when I'm 50 I'm gonna be hard and tough as nails at the rate I live my life. My job keeps me physically fit, I don't have to join some spa and pay someone to lift their dumbbells. Yesterday, I got five blisters on top of callouses I'd already had. When you have that kind of physical pain six or eight times a day, drop a board on your foot, break a toe... I go through at least five times a day where I get hurt bad enough to say 'god damn fucking son of a bitch.'

"How many times a day does the average Joe Blow actually feel physical pain? In a respect that hardens you. You become tough enough not to take shit from anybody, but you also become compassionate and accept a lot of other people stepping on your toes. Takes a lot for a person to disrupt me to strike back, not that I couldn't clean his plow with one blow."

During his various stints attending KU, Nick has studied philosophy and poetry and has had some success publishing poems. Today, after framing a new house, Nick the philosopher/construction worker/poet sits over a pitcher of beer at the Wheel with his old friend Richie Adams, who can only stay a few hours before catching a flight home.

"Didn't I tell you Richie?" says Nick. "The Wheel on Wednesday nights is the place to be. The sorority girls, the prettiest ones, the rich ones, outnumber the guys five to one!"

Richie grins. He's obviously enjoying the scenery. "Yeah, some things never change Nick, especially you. Aren't you ever gonna outgrow these college girls?"

"I hope not... it'll mean I'm dead. You know, you and me are holdouts, Richie. We're still unattached. We're the last strongholds."

"Hey, what about Emma? I live with her you know."

"Well, you're not hitched now are you?"

"No, but..."

"And you consider yourself single?"

"Well... yeah, but don't tell Emma that!"

"Very funny, Richie. Me, I'd love to meet the perfect woman who's beautiful to me and who wants to raise a child and go for it. I held out from the hippie days on. Back then, none of my male friends wanted to get married. I held out forever. All these guys, except you, you geezer, got married and raised families and I still held out. If we have kids now, we'll be old by the time they're 20. Do you ever think of that?"

"I don't think 60's so old, old man. What's your hurry?" says Richie.

"No hurry, it's just kinda tough. I'm living like a bachelor; if my bachelor friends have trouble, they come to me. Life would be so much simpler if I was married and had my kids to take care of and went to bed at 8 and got up the next day to do it again. The people who can't conform that way have problems."

Creedence Clearwater Revival wells from the juke box. Nick taps the end of a screwdriver on the graffiti-chiseled table in time with the music, his tool belt in a heap on the next chair.

"Usually, I doll up a little before I come to the Wheel, try to strike a happy medium. It's the Madison Avenue image types you promote, the dolled-up guys, who have corrupted every-thing, ruined it for us working stiffs out here who may not be quite as doll-like, but we're good, hard-working men and we're out here single! Good God, Richie, you should be jailed for the kind of crap you promote."

"Yeah, and you should be jailed for picking on these inno-cent, young girls."

"Well, if truth be known, I've rarely dated these sorority girls, I just like to pull their chains a little."

"No kidding, Nick. What would they want with an old hippie like you?"

Just then, two Gamma Phi Betas with heartland smiles approach.

"Hey Nick," says the one with shiny hair the color of summer wheat, "How're your birds, Tweedledee and Tweedledum?"

"Hell, they're alright, but they'd be better if you two dropped by again to see 'em. Hey, you gonna take sailing classes again this summer?"

"Depends on whether or not I flunk French, and have to

stick around for summer school," she replies as she gravitates toward the jocks at the other end of the bar.

Turning back to his friend and refilling his beer from the pitcher on the table, Nick asks, "Richie, you gonna marry Emma?"

"I don't know, Nick. I just can't seem to cross that line. It's on my mind a lot, trouble is, I'm of two minds. Emma calls me Sybil." They laugh.

"As I see it, Richie, the essence of the whole deal is your male/female, positive/negative, yin/yang," Nick responds. "It takes two to complete. Two linked together make one. It's that simple. Anyone who denies that is half a bubble off. When you find yourself alone, if you say you're happy, it's only because you have to convince yourself that your way is good, because if you accept less than that, you're not fulfilled and you won't be happy. I'm convinced that most men who say they prefer to be alone probably have such a big ego that no one wanted to be around them. They have to convince themselves that they like being alone."

"I don't like being alone," Richie says, "but it's better than being unhappy with someone. You live alone, Nick, and you don't seem so miserable."

"Well, I'm not completely happy and very rarely do I remember being happy, but at best, I'd be content. I'm reasonably content now, yes," Nick nods. "I meet women and I have a girl-friend, Ellie."

"You meet women *and* you have a girlfriend! Not a bad arrangement, Wild Man. Who's this Ellie?"

"Ellie, yeah, she's a great lady. I met her when I taught sailing class for the KU sailing club. She's getting her master's degree at KU and she has two daughters who are definitely not accepting of a new father figure at their time of life, so that excludes the idea of a marriage proposal. They reject the idea of somebody else moving into their home; their father left eight years ago.

"So, what are you gonna do about these kids?" Richie asks.

"What can I do? If it doesn't work with Ellie because of her protective instinct for her kids, well, I'm cognizant of that phenomenon. I'd hate to lose her as a friend, she's so special. We entertain getting married, but the practicality of it is minimal. I'm a hardcore, masculine entity; that's why I'm a bachelor. A woman can understand me, but a couple of kids, they can't.

"The kids are first in her life. Her education, to become productive, is second in her life. She loves me tooth and nail, but I'm placed third in her life. It's different from a woman who loves a man first before the kids are born, then raises the offspring. So I'm third on the list, and my ego has a difficult time accepting that. I can understand, but I can't accept. I could be first on Someone's list."

Nick's eyes wander across the noisy room to the pool table which is, at this moment, being graced by the lovely pear shape of a co-ed as she bends over to make a difficult shot.

"Interesting shot, eh," Richie chuckles.

"You and I are Scorpios, Richie, and as you know sexuality is our nature. Pisces, well their feet rule them. The genitals rule Scorpio... our brains are below the belt. I love to make love. That's what we're here for after all, to procreate, gotta keep souls moving into bodies. And I do love all women. They're in a society where they're male dominated, but even the ones I feel sorry for, I love them.

"I know what you mean, Nick, but tell me this. How do you reconcile loving all women, to loving one woman? Are you faithful to Ellie?" Richie asks.

"Well, kinda, sorta, I've tried," replies Nick. "I like Ellie enough to kinda think I'm being faithful to her. I've never been that faithful to anyone in my life. Like I said Scorpios' brains are below their belts. I'm trying to make her feel comfortable and happy for now."

The sky darkens, Nick and Richie chug their beers and head for Nick's house. They walk along Massachusetts Street, the town's main drag. Sweet-smelling honeysuckle and redbud trees line the residential streets named Kentucky and Tennessee, their grand old houses sagging after years of abuse from student tenants and negligent landlords. Kids in Pontiac Fieros and Trans Ams cruise Massachusetts, music blaring from open windows.

Nick and Richie round the corner and are surprised by a guest sitting on Nick's front stoop, a lanky, teenage boy wearing black jeans and a Kansas City Royals sweatshirt.

"Hey, Donny, how're ya doing?" Nick says, sitting down on the stoop.

"Hey, Nick, OK. You think you could pick up a bottle of Tequila for me? There's a big party over at Kevin's."

"OK, in a little bit. I'm still talking to my friend here. How old are you, Donny? 16? Did your mother spoil you? I bet she didn't.

"I gotta theory, Richie, that 90 percent of marriages fail because of weaknesses instilled in, I think, the men. They've had a very kind upbringing from the baby boom generation on, the Beaver Cleaver syndrome, a lot of money. Men have been spoiled by their mothers, possibly rejected by fathers, and they fight back egocentrically by taking it out on their women. If they'd worked hard labor for at least a few years, instead of gone to college and had a cushy upbringing... they're so damn dumb at 25, they don't know how to treat their wives. It's a major disruption in the American society. Ain't that right Donny?"

"Jesus, Nick, I don't know what you're talking about. Hey, who are these girls?" Donny asks, as two teenagers walk up the path to the house.

"Dunno, never saw 'em before. What can I do you for, ladies?"

"Would it be all right if we used your bathroom?" the smaller one replies without the least hesitation.

"Sure... Donny here'll show you the way to the facilities."

When the girls leave a few minutes later, Donny leaves with them, apparently foregoing the bottle of Tequila.

"There's a boy's got his priorities straight," Nick grins.

He spoke more quietly then. The whoosh of a ceiling fan from inside the house could be heard. Moths flapped against the glass globe of the porch light.

"I believe spiritually I may be meant to be alone. Some people believe that because they can't accept the defeat. But I don't know, I'm not sure I'm supposed to be married. If that's the case, I really ought to healthfully accept that. I need to accept that. What I'd like to have happen, ideally, is to be conventional, to be married. If I meet a woman who loves me as much as I love her. I know women can get just as egotistically testy as men, but a real strong man is a good man to a woman.

"That's the way this planet was meant to work, male/female, positive/negative. If you don't find that, you're only half what you're capable of becoming, and then, let's face it, you're one sorry son of a bitch."

Nick Wilder's ultimate dream is to buy 20 acres of land in Lawrence, Kansas on which he'd build a house for his wife and children, and to buy his very own sailboat which he'd keep out at Clinton Reservoir.

Mr. Wants-It-All Decides

Scorpio *is* the most sexual sign in the zodiac, Richie muses, sweeping his rented car up Massachusetts Street before heading out of Lawrence. What Nick doesn't realize, it is also the most extreme, the most like a labyrinth, with many ways in and no way out. Despair ye of hope who enter here.

At the Kansas City airport, Richie makes a beeline for United's Frequent Flier Lounge. Something's wrong, and booze won't help. He phones Emma from the Lounge, gets an answering machine. His message is exuberant and brief: "I love you, honey."

He'd said nothing about getting married in weeks. Since the last false start, when he'd told her to meet him at City Hall then backed out, they'd agreed not to talk about it.

"There comes a time, either you get married or you don't. If I wasn't going to marry her, if I wasn't committed, I had no right to her time. I didn't want to get married particularly, but I decided on that flight back to New York that if that's what it takes, that's what it takes."

He doesn't particularly wish not to be married either. Richie's problem is that he can go either way, or neither way, or any way. He's stuck in a spin, round and round in a default mode, in which his only decision is no decision.

Richie's one sure source of control is his career as a copy-writer; he gets to keep his hair long, a symbolic victory, and make his own hours, a real triumph. Despite these advantages, Richie's hot and bothered; most men his age are married, have a couple of kids and their first or second midlife crisis out of the way. But for Richie, the eternal if reluctant bachelor, the midlife crisis is unending. He fears fixity yet longs for it, and forces every woman he's seriously involved with to experience his conflicts about marriage and commitment.

The good part of the bachelor life, the freedom, the excite-ment of meeting new women, has finally been overtaken by the bad, no domestic discipline, failed connections and doubt about his ability to make a relationship last.

In Richie's SoHo loft, the advertiser of packaged goods keeps his spice rack neatly sorted and his foodstuffs apportioned into single sized servings, as if maintaining a household alone, even while he's living with Emma. She'd often felt like a bystander in his single life. He had separate condiments, a separate phone, a separate answering machine and, though he didn't know or couldn't admit it, they were well on their way to separate beds.

Richie may carry himself like a single man, but he wants the security of married life, of sharing his life with one special other, and growing together over the years. He wants the inti-macy that only comes from long-term monogamous relation-ships. He doesn't want to start over with someone new. But is it natural for people to pair up with a single mate for life?

Dressed in black slacks and a grey knit tennis shirt, Richie sits in the VIP Lounge and studies the ladies in their business suits, slacks, skirts. How many of them are married? He scans their hands for wedding rings. He's fascinated by women, and nostalgic for the days when marriage concerned others not him.

Among frequent fliers, he'd logged more miles than most, and he is remarkably comfortable in airports. "Being in transit is about as uncommitted as you can get. In planes, I'm beyond the calamities of living in any one place. Above the clouds at 35,000 feet with a few scotches under my belt, I'm part of everything and nothing." Nursing his alcohol fix, Richie wants what no one can have: both of his lives, all of his worlds, not only the one that begins "for better or worse."

Most of Richie's New York friends are married. Fast-paced executives, a forty-something crowd, they like to remind him he isn't getting any younger. And they all love Emma, just like Richie's family.

Well, they'd see this time: Richie Adams, married man, family man, feet on the ground, rooted, solid, with his one true love "till death do us part." Hallelujah. Amen.

"You know how it is. Before you break up, you have these steamy fantasies. And then when it happens, the reality is you spend the night alone hugging the pillow and feeling so lonely and lost that it hurts. And then comes the dread of having to date new people, or being with people you feel nothing for. Certainly not love. No, I didn't want this. I wanted Emma, I wanted it to be us."

Richie diverts a couple of screaming infants by making amusing sounds and faces. But all he can think about is those young college girls at The Wheel in Lawrence.

"Emma once told me I lacked the instinct for love. It doesn't seem possible. But what if she's right?"

Since he graduated high school in the late sixties, Richie's rallying cry has been, "Routine kills the spirit." It is supposed to inspire change, life as ceaseless renewal, a continual molting of the skin. But Emma, working her quiet magic on him, brought about another kind of change.

A flight attendant with a Pepsodent smile and Ivory Soap skin distracts Richie momentarily. Just another fleeting fantasy now. Emma dispenses the indispensable salve that makes him not creak so much. Not creaking is a lot more important at his age than anything the single life has to offer. Yet his decision is both final and non-binding.

Understandably, Emma will be, at best, skeptical about it. He's the most moody man she'd ever been with. She can leave the house for an hour and when she gets back home his mood has changed entirely. She doesn't know what she's walking into. He is cursed with an overactive brain. He doesn't do, he thinks, and his thinking is endless.

Richie turns Emma's soft indictments over in his hyper-active skull as the 757 descends into the New York area. "The weather pattern diverted the flight path further south than usual and we approached right over my building in SoHo. I had the uncanny sensation I was communing with Emma, down there. I felt warmed to the soul by the thought of her, us, safe and secure inside our nest. But also scared. Afraid that time had run out."

Nick had called Richie a holdout. "What a joke! My old hippie dream of Union with the One and Sex with the Many expired on my trip to Lawrence," Richie says. "I'd never wanted to buy into the all-or-nothing trip but I just couldn't escape it now. Either I grabbed hold of her unequivocally, or she'd be gone forever."

As Richie Adams tells it, he walked off the plane at LaGuardia following behind a fetching Hispanic girl. "'Wake up,' I told myself. 'You're a married man now, embrace your ball and chain.'"

As the cab streaks along Grand Central Parkway toward

the city, he feels liberated, solid, morally sound, connected. He doesn't have to worry about being single again. He doesn't have to face the prospect of weeks, months, maybe even years alone if he and Emma break up. And he'll never have to come home to an empty house again, or wake up alone in a bed much too big for one. He'd put the whole grisly hunt for whatever it was he'd been hunting for behind him. To hell with the life above the clouds, he was going to be rooted, real.

"Yes, ladies and gentlemen, take a good last look at the aging bachelor, soon to turn 40, with wrinkles at the corners of his eyes, a developing prostrate problem and a family history of diabetes and heart trouble, about to take the plunge."

The ad man opens the door to their loft and steps inside. He hears the sound of Emma's footsteps deep within their clean, well-lighted space. As she emerges from the bedroom, he notices a few pieces of luggage lined up against the wall.

"What's this, honey?" Richie asks. His heart drops down into his feet as he gives his "wifey" a hug. He'd hugged her that way a thousand times before, but never with such momentousness.

"'Don't act so surprised, Richie. You're not ready for this,' she says. 'We need to move on. I need to move on.'

"Incredible as it seems to me now, because it all came down the wrong way, I asked her to marry me. I actually said 'This time's for real.' Can you imagine?

"And all she says is, 'I've made up my mind since you couldn't make up yours. Marrying someone isn't a forced march to a labor camp. You don't have the marrying gene, Richie, so let's stop kidding ourselves.'

"I carried her bags. I argued with her, lamely, as we rode the elevator to the street. She wasn't even adamant, she was indifferent. That's when I knew I was sunk."

"Where are you going to stay?"

"With a friend."

Some guy maybe? Richie watched her cab pull away and went back upstairs. And like any self-respecting almost-forty-year-old who'd been dumped on the day he proposed, Richie sat in the dark and drank.

Yeah, Scorpios. Aren't they the ones who sting themselves to death?

Baby Shower

Emma Flynn winced when she saw the invitation. Its pink and blue umbrellas announced a baby shower for Sherry, a long-ago friend who had deserted the singles' playgrounds of Manhattan for the life of a suburban housewife many years ago.

"Uh oh. A baby shower, a *pot luck* baby shower, on a Saturday afternoon. I thought that kind of thing went out in the 50s," Emma mused as she climbed the five flights of stairs to her three-room walk-up in Manhattan's East Village.

Old time's sake and her true affection for Sherry compelled her to accept the invitation, against her better judgment. Two weeks later Emma found herself schlepping an enormous pot of homemade cauliflower soup from her apartment to the train station in Hoboken, New Jersey, wondering all the while why she had made such a ridiculously impractical dish. "Who in their right mind would ride public transportation with a bucket of soup?" she thought as she boarded the Erie Lackawanna.

The train whisked Emma westward through the tall reeds and taller garbage landfills of the New Jersey Meadowlands. She begrudged having to give up this glorious autumn afternoon, envisioning herself trapped in a crepe-paper draped room with unknown married women, forced to play weird, ritualistic shower games. She only hoped her baby gift — a tiny yellow sweater — was appropriate.

Described by her friends as a "free spirit," Emma is 30, but looks younger, with her unruly blond curls and freckled face. She makes her living as an illustrator for an alternative-press magazine located in a low-rent district of Manhattan. The hours are flexible and the standard dress consists of jeans and loose sweaters, the perfect job for Emma.

Something of her Peter Pan outlook on life shows through in her impish grin, but Emma knows all is not well in Never Never Land these days. Emma feels stirrings her friends cannot know. She is struggling silently with conflicts she's convinced even the most footloose among us eventually must face: commitment versus freedom; married versus single; the yen for security versus the alluring potential of the unknown.

"Look," she says. "I hate to let my friends down, but I don't know how much longer this 'free spirit' thing will last. I know I'm a late bloomer, but something happened to me. Something changed when I lived with Richie."

Richie and Emma were drawn to each other by a common love of freedom, of play, of ideas. They found each other fascinating, and eventually they moved in together. After several months, Emma realized she was undergoing a profound change when visions of Richie and her as a family with a baby began creeping into her daydreams, once filled with Technicolor adventures in exotic lands.

"At first I thought, this is so unlike me, so conventionally boring, so damn girlish. But eventually I accepted those urges to nest and propagate. I actually visualized Mother Nature as a wise old broad who had outsmarted me, just like she'll keep outsmarting those like me till the end of time. I began to like the feeling and decided to make it happen."

As fate would have it, Richie felt no such tugs from Mother Nature. That didn't surprise Emma. After all she'd fallen in love with him for his zany irreverence toward convention, his wit, his facile mind.

"Richie and I wracked our brains to try and figure a way we could meet each other's needs, but there was no solution. So eventually, last May, I moved out. It's been really difficult because we're still so close... we talk on the phone all the time, we get together. I know, he knows, we should stop seeing each other, so both of us can move on. But neither of us has any discipline that way. I mean, we turn to each other to help each other get over the other! It's ridiculous."

Although at times she aches physically from the loneliness of missing Richie, Emma admits that she is surprised and somewhat aghast at the lightness and happiness she feels at other times, now that she is on her own again. She has begun to suspect that long-lasting relationships are based on fulfilling mutual needs, not necessarily on love. This insults her romantic view of life, but like all the other things happening to her recently, she accepts it as inevitable. It sure made things simpler: determine your needs and do what you have to do to satisfy them. It was certainly more straight-forward than love, anyway.

Gazing out the train's window at the brilliant foliage in backyards growing progressively larger, Emma wondered what Sherry's marriage was based on. There were certainly no apparent signs of affection between Sherry and her husband, and she knew they'd had a couple of trial separations. What kept them together? Maybe they each feared being alone, maybe they just needed to be a family.

When she arrived at the shower, Sherry wasn't there yet, so

she made her way to the kitchen and put her pot of soup on the back burner, while other women unwrapped plates of cold cuts, cheese cubes and chip dip.

"I'd promised myself not to be cynical, but I couldn't help noticing that the women in the kitchen were a drab-looking bunch. They looked tired and round shouldered. You know, they had over-permed hair and smoked cigarettes. I felt conspicuously over-dressed. They all seemed to be about my age, related to Sherry by blood or marriage. Every one of them was married, and must have had kids because that's all they talked about. I felt conspicuously single."

Emma made a few unsuccessful stabs at conversation, but could not penetrate the many levels of family gossip. She sat on the living room couch with a couple of sweet octogenarians waiting for Sherry to arrive. She glanced at her watch and wondered what her friends in Manhattan were doing at that moment. She felt she could not have been further from her life on East 5th Street if she'd been on the moon.

At last Sherry waddled in behind her stomach, as clear-eyed and pretty as ever, Emma was glad to see. "I wondered how Sherry's wacky way of looking at life was reconciled to all this. Was she doing a beautiful job of faking it? Had she become one of them? Was she simply doing what she had to do?"

With the guest of honor's arrival, lunch became the focus of attention as everyone served themselves buffet style. Emma's cauliflower soup was ignored, until finally one of the older women was polite enough to ladle out a bowl full of the creamy green concoction. She proclaimed it to be delicious, and soon a dozen women were raving about it and asking Emma for the recipe.

"I don't know why, but I felt so relieved. They like me... yeah! (They like my soup anyway.) Before the soup success I felt like such an oddball there, sort of lonely. Now, on some level, I was OK; these married women accepted me. I got through the rest of the lunch and then gift-opening time was announced. Hot dog, I thought, the end is near."

Sherry faced an enormous pile of gifts, wrapped in pastel paper secured by elaborate bows, her guests seated in a circle on couches and folding chairs. Time went by painfully slowly with all the oohing and ahhing over each gift, passed from lap to lap around the room. The endless uttering of pleasantries nearly drove Emma to distraction. She longed to hear one of Richie's irreverent asides.

"What that shower needed was a few men! I was really bored and sat there wondering whether motherhood was for me. Later I decided it's the trappings that make me so antsy. I mean a baby shower is an impossibly contrived, social situation we are duped into for practical reasons. That's what Richie says about marriage, too. I can see what he means."

At last, when all the gifts were opened, Emma took her leave. She both pitied and envied Sherry as she kissed her goodbye. She hoped her new baby would be healthy.

Emma refused a ride back to the train station, saying that she'd rather walk. It was dark, the moon was full and the air was clean and cold. She smelled the smoke of wood burning fires and felt deliriously happy to be alone.

"For some reason I wanted to do something wild and objectionable... break windows, write graffiti on the train station... except, of course, I never did those things."

Instead she set her sights on the neat mounds of leaves piled in the gutter in front of each house. As she zigzagged her way to the train station, she gave each pile a good, hard kick, setting hundreds of leaves free under the moonlit sky.

* * *

On Monday morning, Emma sat perched on the high stool before her drawing board, sipping coffee and trying to become fully awake. The office was an airy, open loft space with huge windows spanning the south wall. Industrial-sized ceiling fans and a few bright banners dangled from the high ceilings, crisscrossed by a vast network of exposed pipes and electrical conduits. Six or seven people worked in the large room, and though they were from diverse backgrounds, they shared an easy camaraderie.

Emma was thinking back to her ordeal on Saturday, and she was baffled. "There I was surrounded by the results of couple-dom and baby stuff, the things I thought I wanted, and what was my reaction? All I wanted was to escape and do something naughty... go figure."

She gazed across the loft and watched Dolores Castrodad, the company's receptionist, busily going through her morning routine of opening the mail. What a sweet girl, Emma thought. She's too young to have so many problems: two kids, never enough money, no husband — only that guy Tony who keeps jerking her around. I bet she didn't have any cutesy baby shower at her apartment in the Bronx when Maria was born. She's a child raising children really, though she's older than me in many ways.

Waiting for Him

"Tony knew I had an abortion, but he didn't want me to talk about that other baby," Dolores Castrodad tells us emotionally, in her clipped Hispanic accent. "He was living with her by then. This baby was pretty big. He was six months inside me. God, I just wanted to die. I had to go through natural labor. The only thing is, he was dead when he came out because they injected salt in me to kill him. I had to go into the hospital. I didn't know I was pregnant. I was very irregular. We would do our thing and I would get pregnant. I would try to be careful, but sometimes you get into a situation and... you know how it is.

"I used birth control but I guess I didn't use it right. The thing is my mother never taught me these things. She never gave me any advice.

"I suffered a lot. I thought I was gonna die. Because in the hospital when you abort a baby that big, they leave you alone with that baby so you can look at it so you can feel guilty. They make believe they are just going out to do something. But they don't. They leave you there. I saw it. I could see his hands. I think it was going to be a boy. I saw two little balls, very tiny. I picked him up. I touched it. It looked like — picture me without skin. All those veins. But I still loved it. I loved that baby even though it looked like that. I touched him and put it in the palm of my hand. And I dropped it when the doctor came in. And I felt so bad, I dropped it. And when the doctor went out, I picked it back up."

She told Tony, "It was going to look just like you. It had your little nose."

"Shut up," he said, "I don't want to hear that. I don't want to talk about that."

"I would try to talk about it with Tony. I wanted him to feel the pain that I suffered. When they put me back into the room, I cried for a long time, for the whole afternoon and the whole night. I was thinking about when they injected that salt into me, and how he died and whether he was choking. I'm human and he was human, and I was just thinking about that. That's painful. After that, I came home and I thought I would never get over it. Every time I saw a movie with a baby or a baby in the street, I never thought I would forgive myself for what I'd done. But I have to forgive myself, or God will never forgive me.

"Sometimes I do hate Tony for what he's done. I wanted that baby. I had to make that decision for the other baby because I couldn't cope with another kid. All three of them would have suffered in the cold or rain, or fall down the stairs if the elevator was broken."

Dolores Castrodad was born 24 years ago in Puerto Rico, the illegitimate daughter of a woman who came to New York to escape her reputation as the village "puta." Dolores claims her mother wasn't a whore at all. She was just "very friendly, and oh so good looking."

Dolores's diminutive, well-padded body, flushed cheeks, and shy sensuality give the impression of a Puerto Rican cupid. The dark eyes in her baby face reflect eagerness to please and sincerity. Just beneath the surface hover hurt and vulnerability. She seems incapable of guile or bitterness which is astounding, considering the rotten hand life has dealt her so far.

She grew up in a Hispanic area of the Bronx in a series of welfare hotels and subsidized apartment buildings. Her friendly mother was more interested in the dozens of cats she kept than in Dolores. And although she's never met her natural father who lives in Puerto Rico, she was all too familiar with the series of step-fathers who railroaded through her young life. When she was 19, she moved in with the family of her boyfriend Tony in order to escape the sexual attacks of her then step-father. While she and Tony lived with his mother, they had two children. They never married, and a year ago Tony moved out to go live with his new girlfriend, Nancy.

Dolores found herself single, with two babies, no job, no man, no education, and no home. In spite of everything, she continues to love Tony with a devotion and passion verging on adoration. She finds she is not able to love another man.

After Tony left her, Dolores managed to secure a job as receptionist for the magazine where Emma Flynn works. She moved into a two-room apartment in the Bronx with her two kids whom she leaves with a neighbor, before she catches the IRT to work each morning. Dolores has never had the luxury of taking life anything but dead seriously, and she approaches it with a fatalistic determination. It is the particular combination of vulnerability and determination in such a cherubic looking girl/woman that makes Dolores so appealing, so likeable.

On the same sunny Saturday in October that Emma attends the baby shower, Dolores is home with her children. She sits on one of two plastic lawn chairs in her 15th floor, two-room apartment in the Bronx. Except for the bunk beds, there is no other furniture in the room. This is her children's bedroom/ playroom/ TV room. The walls, covered in pre-school scribble, were decorated by the kids and their Crayolas. Pee Wee Herman's squeaky voice and surreal world flash across the TV screen. Maria, age 4, and T.J., age 2, play with a pile of plastic toys on the floor.

As she sips orange juice from a Garfield the Cat glass, Dolores describes Tony's new girlfriend, "You see Nancy's 28... she's been out in the world before me. She went to college. She's had several jobs, you know as a waitress and an account executive. She's mature. She's met a lot of people, so I guess she has some things to talk about. She's American, and you know Americans tend to go out to a lot of places. That's what Tony was looking for, someone smart who has a lot to talk about."

The kids have set up plastic bowling pins, and Dolores lifts her feet as bowling balls come hurtling under her chair.

"My friends tell me to go out with someone else, so OK I do, with Manny, the security guard in our building. But I find in him so many faults. Like I was telling my brother, he's too skinny, his teeth go out like this, and his hair goes like that, and he's not a Tony. And I know I'm never going to find another Tony.

"And that Manny, for a few days we were kissy, kissy, because I miss that. He says 'You're so beautiful, I wish you were mine.' You see, you need to hear those things, but see, I need to hear that from Tony not from someone else. That's how my heart feels. I don't want nobody touching me but Tony."

A screech emerges from roly-poly T.J. as a plastic bowling pin lands smack on the top of his head. He crawls into Dolores's soft lap. "Oh, Papi, no llores. It's OK. Dejame tocarte. It's OK. Shhhhh."

Dolores and T.J. are momentarily mesmerized by Sylvester the Cat chasing Tweety Bird round and round on the color TV screen. T.J.'s sobs quiet down as his thumb finds its groove in his little mouth.

"Tony sometimes stays here, and we sleep together. Because he doesn't get what he wants from her. He loves me also. He lets me know. He tells me 'I don't want to do this, I don't want to hurt you.' And when we finish he feels guilty. He doesn't want to hurt me.

"Friday, he stayed over and we did our thing. Now Tuesday, he'll come over. I don't know what time he'll come or how long he'll stay. He's smart. See, if he comes Tuesday, and knows he won't see me till Sunday, he'll try to get me into bed. I'm trying to figure out why he does it. I try to understand him, to see what he sees. Sometimes I feel happy, sometimes I feel used. Sometimes I feel cheap, sometimes I feel loved.

"If he spends the night over here, he tells her he spends the night with his mother. Of course, he lies to me, too. He has to. He has to lie to her and he has to lie to me because that way she won't get hurt and I won't get hurt. I understand that. That way it doesn't cause me pain.

"He told me I will always be his Number One. I was his first. He will never trust anyone the way he trusts me. Because I've shown him that he can trust me. He even tells me things about her. Sometimes she's a pain, and she wants more out of him, for him to meet her friends. He doesn't want to, he's lazy. He would like to meet other girls, too. But he's lazy. He told me he stays with her because he needs help paying the rent. Gosh, he's fresh," Dolores laughs.

Dolores and Tony talk more now, are becoming better friends than when they lived together. She has become his confidante;

he has become her advisor, regarding work and people out in the big world. Enmeshed in what would seem to be an impossibly painful situation, these two are making their way in unchartered territory.

"If he decides to come back, or if he asks me, and that won't happen for years... I feel it, he won't come back for years. I'm willing to wait. Unless, I guess if I meet someone else. But until I get him out of my system, I won't meet someone else.

"With Manny, I proved to myself that I can go out with someone, but I proved to myself that I love Tony because I can't make a commitment to Manny. Jesus, he's so skinny. And Tony's hair is not good like mine, but it's not bad. And Manny's hair is bad. I like to feel good hair, like mine, like T.J.'s. Manny's is too kinky, and he's skinny and he smokes. I find so many faults. He's not my Tony." She laughs at that thought. A ruckus is underway across the room.

"OK, Maria, tu coje uno y tu coje el otro, T.J." The kids are fighting over a pair of Dolores's high heels. Maria insists on having both of them. "¿Por que tu no te conformas con el que tu tienes? Come on Maria, be a big girl."

"I feel more at ease now. Sometimes on Saturdays I wonder if they went out or whatever. But just sometimes, not that much anymore. I try not to think about it because it hurts a lot.

"On Saturdays I like to watch the A Team, Knight Rider, Star Trek, and Friday the 13th Monsters. So that keeps me busy. So I don't think about them. On Sundays though there's nothing on TV so I wonder what they're doing. I guess I want him to have fun with me, not with someone else.

"But you know I love him and what can I do? I try to think positive. One time, when I found out he was living with her, I got to the point of jumping into the river, but what stops me is

God put these two kids in the way, because He knows I would throw myself off the bridge if I didn't have these kids. But I don't want anyone else to take care of my kids because I know what they need, and when they go to school I want to be there for their little shows, and at Christmas and Halloween. I love them, and I know they're gonna miss me and need me. So that's what stops me. I went through so much pain, but I guess I don't have it that bad."

Dolores was raised in a patriarchal society where she was taught to be submissive and loyal to her man, come what may. Through her job, Dolores is starting to establish at least a modicum of economic independence for herself and her children. Encouragement and support from her co-workers have begun to give her a sense of self-worth, apart from Tony, apart from her kids. Unlike Emma Flynn who determines what she wants and has the freedom and confidence to act on it, Dolores's choices are limited. Circumstances have tied her hands tightly.

Monday afternoon at the office, Emma notices that Dolores is breathless with pleasure and anticipation. Into the office strolls her lunch date, a good-looking, well-built Puerto Rican man, slightly embarrassed as Dolores steers him into the center of the loft to present him to her co-workers.

"Everybody," she beams, "I want you to meet Tony, the father of my children."

After lunch, she dreamily reports that he took her downstairs to McDonalds where she had a Big Mac and a chocolate shake.

Socially Aware Jewish Woman Seeks Man

In a fashionable West Side bar where beautiful people have "positive cognitive experiences," Emma's ex finds himself sitting with a woman he imagines every man in the bar, gay or straight, would find unattractive. She *is* homely, with her thick glasses, and dowdy clothes that make her look like a middle-aged spinster. She is cautiously witty and optimistic, but obviously very sensitive about her looks. Seeing that, Richie takes pains not to hurt her feelings.

In the months since he and Emma broke up, Richie hasn't been able to connect with another woman. Funny, when he was with Emma, he imagined connecting with all women. Now, nothing. Nada. Hell, he didn't even have the will to try to meet new people, but he figured he had to do something. So, partly from boredom, partly from wishful thinking, he'd answered a personal ad.

Her ad read, "My friends say I'm attractive," which should have been the tipoff, but he needed to believe she'd be his life raft. Had he read between the lines, he'd have picked up her desperate hope to be: Attractive. Desired. Accepted. Instead of homely and alone, placing an ad in the neighborhood weekly for "a good, decent man, 25 to 40, who takes social justice and mental health seriously. I make a great post-sixties vegetable soup for male with humor and nuance."

Comparing the person he is sitting with to the one in the ad, his disappointment is palpable. She'd referred to her "shapely form" but she's overweight. Her ad made her sound sensible, accessible, and now he knows why.

Dear Westsider Box 997:

I really liked your ad. My friends also say I'm attractive. I'd better take their word for it; I have a distorted self-image. I've been called a cross between Kevin Costner and Dustin Hoffman. I like your shapely form as much as your feminist politics. Let's get together and see if we can progress as far as vegetable soup. I make a mean salad.

She's also disappointed. She'd hoped for more. She'd hoped for someone more sincere. His letter made him seem understanding, slow to judge or condemn. Now he seems so typical. Another man who wants women to look like models in magazine ads. She senses he's disappointed too.

"I'll be wearing a red scarf and black coat," she said on the phone. She had a throaty, raspy voice he liked. Now that he knows what it's wrapped up in, it no longer excites him. On the phone, she told him she wore glasses, "for distance." That she felt the need to add "for distance" would have been endearing, if she had turned out to be as attractive as advertised.

It's raining and Amsterdam Avenue is slick; impressionistic smudges of green and red traffic lights shimmer on the road. He arrives at the appointed meeting spot earlier than her. A good sign. The better looking she is, the later she'll arrive, he tells himself. Sitting next to a wall of photographs of women dressed in black, he finally notices a girl in — oh no — red scarf and black coat, coming into the bar.

Maybe she won't see me, he thinks. Should I pretend to be someone else? Ooops, she's putting on her glasses... for distance. He's sunk.

She sounds out his opinion about everything from *New York Magazine* to the new Carnegie Hall, realizing she wouldn't have been interested in him if she'd met him casually. When she asks what he does, he launches into an interminable account about how he joined the Peace Corps in the seventies and spent two years in Brazil where he got hepatitis and almost died.

It is painfully obvious they can't connect. She tries to think of a way she can excuse herself early. It's poetic justice, he muses. With looks such an important thing, what do I get? Someone who's my idea of homely. The kind of girl I was too good for growing up and here I am, sitting with her in a crowded bar on a Friday night.

As she compares the Kandinsky show to the John Singer Sargent exhibition, he fantasizes that he can learn to love a mousy Jewish girl in her thick tortoise shell glasses, but it's no use. Attraction can't be learned.

"I've got to get going," she says. "I have an early day tomorrow."

"Okay," he says. "I'll pay the check. I could walk you home."

Is he being polite? In the street, he offers her his arm. Richie walks her six blocks in the rain to her apartment building on 72nd Street. It starts to pour. They're getting drenched.

"Would you like to come up, just until it stops?" she asks.

A few moments later, she puts her key in the door and pushes it open. She has a lovely place, he thinks, stepping in.

Epilogue

Emma Flynn married an architect in 1994 and had three children including a set of twins. The marriage lasted 9 years. Single ever since, Emma says she is happy and at peace with her children, friends and career. She is not seeking a mate, but is open to the possibility. She continues to work as a freelance magazine illustrator in New York City.

Richie Adams can bend your ear with epic stories from his globe-trotting years in advertising (he's a retired 'brand consultant' now living in Connecticut). But what he doesn't talk about much is his personal or family life. He was married for more than a decade, and says he was devastated by the divorce. That was five years ago. He tries to date now and then, but mostly can't be bothered. In his mid-sixties, he's working his way through his wine cellar. The pain he feels in being so alone is momentarily lessened, he says, by a good red.

About a year after she was interviewed, Dolores Castrodad stole $17,000 from the company where she and Emma worked. She tore a check from the middle of the company checkbook and forged her boss's name. By the time the theft was discovered, Dolores was long gone. The company never pressed charges.

Nick Wilder is out there somewhere, but we weren't able to locate him.

III. THE WORLD IS WHAT YOU MAKE IT

"The mind is its own place, and in itself
Can make a heav'n of hell, a hell of heav'n."
John Milton, *Paradise Lost*

Look Before You Leap (Then Jump Anyway)

Evie Sachs coldly studied Michael from her vantage point in front of the large picture window facing south on 23rd Street in Manhattan. The bright midday light poured in from behind her, causing Michael, with five o'clock shadow at eleven a.m., to squint as he looked at her. His squinting gave her a tiny rise of satisfaction. Standing there, sulking, he looked like a small boy who had been trampled in football scrimmage by a squad of much larger boys. He bullied her with lies and deceit and here he is looking bullied.

"Don't give me that hurt sheepdog look," she said. "If you can smuggle rands out of South Africa, I guess you can find a place to stay."

"Will you give me money so I can get back to Mexico City?"

"No."

"Will you send me to Mauritius so I can get my gold?"

"No. Call one of your gangster friends and have them give you money."

Michael retreated to the kitchen to make a few calls. For a moment, she felt sorry for him. He really didn't have a lot of choices. After a while he drifted back into the living room. A friend in Austin was willing to take him in.

"Good, is he sending you a plane ticket?"

"Well, I have to call him back later."

She figured it this way: "My phone bill is going to be astronomical. Here I am, buying breakfast, lunch and dinner for this guy. I turned to him and said, 'I'll get you a one-way ticket to Austin.'

"I went down to the Liberty Travel, I bought a one-way ticket to Austin for $89, I made love to him one more time, gave him $20 for the airport and that was the end of that."

He called a couple of times, and the third time collect. "I refused to accept the charges. It had nothing to do with the money. I wanted him to know that I'm not here for him anymore."

Lucky Evie... not only does she get a gangster on the rebound, but a gangster with no money.

* * *

Evie Sachs is gregarious, outgoing, and inclined to give the benefit of a doubt. She relishes life as an adventure, but she's a tiny raft on rough seas. A people person who usually remains friends with former boyfriends, of whom there are more than a few, Evie's generous to a fault, a trifle naive, and she feels for people.

She hates being described as cute. Even worse, as cuddly. She describes herself, not unfairly, as "sexy, bright, attractive." Her short, shiny brown hair makes a tidy frame for a face called "adorable" enough times to make it to her "most hated adjectives" list. She has large green eyes flecked with gold, an olive complexion and an excited way of talking.

Evie has an abiding respect for people who take chances,

ask the most of themselves. She admires artists, entrepreneurs, explorers. That she doesn't want to settle also accounts for one of her most charming attributes, her spontaneity.

Evie is a party girl with a new wave flair for torn sweat-shirts and jeans (when not wearing Chanel suits). She might be considered oversexed, but by what measure, and whose? Evie's one of those lucky women who can add a couple of pounds here and there and still look good. And she's flirtatious, a quality that comes in handy in her advertising career.

Her idea of love? "Growing and sharing together, being a real team." Her ideal in a man? "He should be spirited. And I've learned this in thirty one years: you need love, but you can't be needy."

The month before Evie's melodramatic farewell scene with Michael, she flew down to the Caribbean. She was coming off the worst year of her life and she needed a break. She'd been engaged, married and divorced in less than a year, and when it came time to get unmarried, "I was the only Jewish girl from Roslyn who had to pay the man."

It was December. Very cold. Snowing. At least the peach-walled condo she and her husband had shared in Manhattan's Chelsea section was still hers. Now that she was single again, she took another step toward mental health. She quit her fast-paced job in advertising. She was ready to start over, from scratch.

Her parents, who'd paid for the condo she and her short-lived marriage mate shared, were off to Cancun for Christmas and New Year's. She asked them if she could get a free vacation out of it and they said yes.

"There were 10,000 Jews in Cancun on vacation, very commercial. They're the worst to be around 'cause they get up at six a.m. and put a sneaker on every chaise lounge, so by 10 a.m. you can't get a chaise lounge anywhere near the pool."

On a day trip to Cozumel, she met Michael. "He was sitting at a bar reading an American paper and I asked him where he got it. He was gorgeous! I joined him for a beer and we sat there and talked for about two hours. I didn't want to leave."

She'd forgotten about the newspaper she'd wanted. She was too busy taking inventory. "Michael was forty years old, he'd been at Goldman Sachs for fifteen years and he'd packed it all in and gotten married and divorced, just like me, in eleven months.

"He'd gone to Boston University like I did, got his masters at Columbia, where I'd put in a short stint, and like those things make you think, 'Oh my God, it's meant to be!' He was pretty busy in Cozumel, writing a book about his bookie father, and building a hotel and a dive shop.

"Plus, he was Jewish! So he had like all the things that somebody like me is looking for, a creative spirit, entrepreneurial, fun, a chance taker, a risk taker, it was just wonderful!" It was a romantic opportunity she didn't dare pass up, not at the age of thirty-one following a divorce.

The next day, Michael called Evie at the hotel. "He said he couldn't stop thinking about me and could he come over for lunch the following day? I said fine. Well, my mother then kicks into being the pain in the ass that she can be in the most adorable way."

Sitting in the chaises about 10 that morning, which Mom reserved with sneakers at six, Mrs. Sachs started in. "Is that him, Evie? I think it's him."

"No, it's not him," said Evie.

Ten minutes later. "Evie, is that him? He looks like he's looking for somebody."

"Mom, it's not him and you're making me nervous, would you please stop?"

When he finally showed up, Evie, Michael, Mom and Dad sat down for drinks by the pool. "Michael talked a mile a minute and was very entertaining, but he sounded like he was brought up on the streets." He didn't have the vocabulary and diction the Roslyn girl was used to "but it was kind of nice."

Michael was "a diamond in the rough" and she was grateful when her parents left her alone with him. They had a couple of drinks and then Michael suggested that they go off somewhere. "He took me to this secluded place, I can't remember the name, a deserted beach, a fish market, a tiny, out of the way hotel. It was very romantic. We were the only English-speaking people there. We just sat there, ate fresh fish and sucked down beers. My parents didn't see me for three days."

After spending New Year's Eve with Michael, she flew back to New York. "I thought, this is it. Everything's gonna turn around. I had a shitass year. And God's watching over me, this is great, gonna be wonderful, I'm so excited.

"The last thing Michael said to me was, 'Go home, get your affairs in order, I'll come visit you in January, I'll spend a coupla weeks, and if we get along the way I think we're gonna get along, we'll come back to the Caribbean, we'll get married and have babies.' And I thought, 'Oh, I know! I can write romance novels and sit in the sun.'"

For three days and nights they'd enjoyed each other. Later, back in New York, she told her friends about never leaving their hotel room. That wasn't quite true. They'd made love on the beach. Walking hand in hand, laughing, looking like the idyllic lovers in those Caribbean beach ads.

* * *

In New York, Evie was floating on air. What luck to have met Michael, and to fall so fast. A few weeks out of the box after her divorce, and a second marriage, a better marriage, was in the offing. For the first time in more than a year, she felt whole. She wasn't hurting. "I felt good about myself, like I'd pulled through."

Michael, a big gambler who talked sports, sports, sports, planned to arrive in New York the day before Super Bowl Sunday. But when he called from Mexico City a week early, he said he couldn't wait any longer and was catching the next flight.

"I ran right out that afternoon and spent $200 on lingerie. An ex-boyfriend of mine owns a limo company. I called him and said, 'Roger, you've got to do me a solid.' He says, 'What do ya need, baby?' 'I need a limo. A nice big stretch limo and a cold bottle of champagne in the back and I need it at less than cost.'"

He says, "Evie, ya got it!"

It was January, and a bad snowstorm in New York delayed the plane in Mexico City. On the phone Michael told her to cancel the limo. "Just leave the door unlocked," he said.

"Great," Evie said. "Meet me between the sheets."

Michael walked in at two in the morning. It was a Thursday, "and we spent Thursday, Friday, Saturday, Sunday, and Monday in bed. I think the dog got walked maybe twice."

She finally got out of bed, only to fly to Florida for a previously arranged job interview. She left Michael in her apartment taking care of her Yorky and the plants. On the flight down, she mulled things over. "We were having a great time, but there were a few things that struck me as weird: Like how come, if he'd been in New York with Goldman Sachs for fifteen years, he hadn't called anyone to say, 'Hi, I'm in town.' How come he has no friends? I mean here I was about to pack up and go down to Cozumel with this guy. You have to find something. You usually don't find the bellbottoms until three months into the relationship. 'Oh my god, he wears bellbottoms, I can't possibly stay with him any longer.' But I only had a limited amount of time to find something wrong with this guy.

"Why hasn't he called anyone? Why aren't we going out to dinner? O.K., fine, maybe it's just wonderful lust and we're gonna stay in the apartment the rest of our lives, but something made me think."

Her first night in Miami, she checked into her hotel and went right to bed. The second night, she spoke to Michael on the phone for three hours. The third night, the man who had interviewed her asked her to have dinner with him.

"He's this big huge shyster of a guy named Rourke and I get into his car to go to dinner with him. I reach into the glove compartment to get a match to light my cigarette and... he's got a gun, a knife and handcuffs in there. Now any normal woman would have gotten scared and demanded to be taken back to her hotel, right?" Not Evie. "I always wanted to fire a gun. I had this overwhelming curiosity. So I asked him to take me to the shooting range."

Rourke was trying to put the moves on her, so he was delighted to teach her to shoot. "There I am, firing off the 38 and the 44 and I'm eyeing the magnum. Come on, let me fire that cannon. If Magnum P.I. can do it, so can I!"

It's amusing now, but Rourke was coming on too strong. "Over dinner, he's talking about his miserable marriage and how he never gets laid by his wife. I'm not in the mood to deal with this. He asked me, 'If I give you the job, you got anything keeping you in New York?'

"I really played up Michael. 'Rourke, it's funny. I just met this guy I'm nuts about.' I told him everything, including the bit about the hotel and dive shop, at which point Rourke put down his silverware. He turned to me and he said, 'Evie, I was in the CIA for nine years and, believe me, something's off here.'

"Now come on, when does a girl from Roslyn get to meet a CIA agent? Never, never. I've never known a CIA person, I've never known a cop. I've never known a fireman personally, I mean it just doesn't happen. And it was almost like cosmic, it really was, because somewhere I really think somebody is looking out for me."

Rourke was the one looking out for her. He told her the dive shops in Cozumel were more famous for laundering money than for refilling oxygen tanks. "So I think, 'Oh my god, Michael's working for his daddy, the bookmaker, and he didn't even tell me!'" She smiled and, just for a lark, asked Rourke to run a check on him. Rourke, more than happy to oblige, made a few calls from his car phone, and a few more from Evie's hotel room. When he put down the phone he said, "Do you know that this guy is under grand jury investigation?"

Michael told her early on he'd been investigated "as a matter of course" at Goldman Sachs. Half her friends on Wall Street were under investigation for one thing or another.

"Do you know that he has a record? Do you know that he's been in jail a couple of times?"

Now she was really scared. "Rourke leaves and I am twitching. *Twitching.* I'm afraid I'm going to walk into my apartment, my dog is going to be dead, my furniture and jewelry are going to be gone and I'm twitching!"

When she got back to her apartment in New York, she confronted Michael right away. She remembers she poured herself a stiff scotch, turned to him and said, "Are you working for your dad?"

"I don't know what you're talking about, Evie. Why would I work for my dad?"

She told him about the CIA guy, that he'd run a check on Michael. "Michael, there's no record of you ever being at Goldman Sachs."

"I worked for people at Goldman Sachs, but I was never really Goldman Sachs," he confessed.

She took another large swig on her scotch. "Did you graduate from Columbia or BU?"

Nothing.

"Michael, do you have a record?"

"Evie," he finally said. "I was gonna tell you."

What he hadn't told her until now was that he'd been busted for bookmaking, international foreign currency fraud, racketeering and gambling. And he'd served four terms "in one of those country clubs where they send white collar criminals."

"For some sick, weird reason I stopped being nervous at that moment. I knew in the back of my mind that there was something strange about this guy, not calling friends and all, I felt relief now that I knew what it was about.

"It was kind of exciting being with somebody that bad. I'd never been with anybody that bad. I went with nice little Jewish boys from Great Neck who like on their worst night, they did an eighth ounce of cocaine. I mean, I never knew anybody that bad. So we talked about it, laughed about it, and made love."

If she was not yet out of his grip, it had less to do with Michael the man than with the idea of Michael. Now that she was in his confidence, he let her in on another secret. He told her he had $200,000 in gold krugerrands stashed in Mauritius. "All I had to do was buy us two tickets to Mauritius. We'd go pick up the krugerrands and hightail it to the Caribbean, have babies and live happily ever after."

Michael outlined an enticing scheme. "Since South African Jews were not allowed to remove their money from the country, we were going to do it for them. Michael and I would fill up suitcases with krugerrands and, using our American passports, smuggle them to Mauritius.

"Michael figured I'd be the greatest beard he'd ever had, and I figured, 'Hey, it's an adventure.'"

Her sister came by the next day and Evie told her the whole story. "It became resoundingly clear that my mother had raised two sociopaths. Sis thought this was like the coolest thing in the world. She couldn't wait to assist Bonnie and Clyde in their adventures in Mauritius. 'Whatever you need, whatever you want, whatever it takes, I'll be there.'"

Perhaps it was her sister's enthusiasm that showed her the folly of her own. Michael had his sights set on Belize as his future banana republic, where he planned to take their gold. Evie's role was to entertain a petty official of Belize to enlist his cooperation.

"Suddenly it all became so absurd. Michael arranged a meeting with a woman who repped Caribbean real estate. He didn't know a damn thing, he didn't even know what a P&L was. I carried us through that meeting, and it became crystal clear that what I had here was not some slick schemer but a total inarticulate asshole. And all of a sudden it was NO! THIS SIMPLY WON'T DO!"

Her sister thought she was crazy, shooing off the scam. "Bored housewives never get to do these things. You'll be sorry when you wind up with another accountant for a husband," Sis warned.

Had Evie been so intent on moving on after her divorce that she'd run all the red lights? Or was it Michael, telling her all the things he knew a woman like her wanted to hear? Had she been that eager and easy to read the afternoon they met in Cozumel? Would she have acted any differently had she known the truth from the beginning? Apart from her questions about her own role in the affair, there was the respect she'd lost for him, not because he was a crook, but because he was a *failed* crook. Instead of James Bond, she'd wound up with a bit player in a Kojak rerun. The successful entrepreneur she'd been attracted to turned out to be a swindler down on his luck. So the sweet illusion ended. The diamond in the rough turned out to be a rhinestone. But Evie is unrepentant. "Does this story make me sound like a jerk?" asks Evie, more than a year later. "No, it makes me sound like a free spirit who's willing to take a chance."

Epilogue

Evie continued to take chances, working her way through a succession of affairs in New York and later Chicago, where she'd moved to get away from a respected Manhattan entrepreneur whom she described three ways: Jealous, paranoid, violent. When we lost touch with her long ago she'd gotten her advertising career back on track and was enjoying Midwestern life. She was living with a Michelin chef within six months of touching down at O'Hare Airport. But where is she today? We located a friend of Evie's who reached out to her on our behalf. Since we never heard back from Evie, we assume that she chose to remain a mystery.

Bodyguard

Emerging from her morning dreams, Heather James slowly gets out of bed and walks to the window. She parts the gingham curtains and squints as she takes in the East End's fine old homes in their green yards and quiet streets. In this town of Muncie, Indiana, from which Dan Quayle hails, Heather owns a large and cluttered 150-year-old Victorian complete with gables, nooks, verandas, gazebos, and a three-story brick chimney. When it went up for sale, Heather pounced on it, for under $50,000.

Since that day she's spent endless hours working on its authentic restoration, poring over architectural plans, getting financing, hiring contractors. Doing proud the town dubbed "Hometown U.S.A." by the local Chamber of Commerce.

Many generations of Jameses have lived in Muncie, also known as Middletown since the Middletown Studies in the fifties proclaimed Muncie the transcendental representation of Middle America. Heather's interest in Victorian renovation was stirred by her grandfather. A seed store proprietor during the Civil War, he'd spent the 1890s making sketches of Muncie's landmark structures.

We first met Heather north of Albany, in New York State,

where she was on assignment for *The Muncie Star*. She was part of a press trip to Lake Placid, winding up in Schenectady, whose historic district she planned to write about.

On her trip, she'd met a handsome reporter named Bob Manning. She liked him, or might have if he hadn't been so quick to ingratiate himself. It wasn't his masculine features but his swagger that got her defenses up. He was sort of the lady killer type she instinctively guarded herself against.

"When I got back to Muncie, I couldn't stop thinking about him. I don't mind saying it, I dreamed about him. In my dreams it's me and Bob, at an inn in Lake Placid," she says. "Cozied up together. Then I wake up and I'm all alone in my 150-year-old Victorian," that lacks but one thing: a family to go with her authentically wainscoted parlors and family rooms, children to play in her garden.

Heather tends her rose garden, one of the city's quiet wonders. Her trip to "the Empire State," opened her eyes, alas, to more than she bargained for. "I learned one more time how unwilling I am to take a chance, to let anyone get close to me." Intimacy is too big a threat to Heather who has the failsafe repellent, "a perfect way to keep men off."

As the reporter walks along Courthouse Square and Walnut Street Plaza, she kicks herself for what happened in New York. Muncie, a/k/a Middletown, is America's Average City. Its residents are not well traveled. Many have never been further away than Indianapolis, about an hour's drive across flat farmland. Ball State University is the major industry, making Muncie a college town. The downtown area has one movie, a pizza place and bars that serve wine and popcorn, no mixed drinks. Randomly deposited here by a Greyhound Bus and not told where you are, you might think of it as "Anywhere, U.S.A." It's a comfortable and claustrophobic provincialism that feels both familiar and foreign to outsiders.

If you live in Muncie, you're supposed to be driven by two things: work and family. In the fifties, after the war, grudging accommodation was made to single people (bachelor apartments and more restaurants), but Muncie is still a city devoted to the institution of marriage; they marry young and try to stay together. Not only does Heather James, a fifth generation Muncieite, not have a family to go with her house, she doesn't have a man she can conceivably love. Not since a grade school crush, and a fling when she was in Ball U. (big joke, that one), has she felt that sort of romance possible.

"At twenty-nine, I'm hardly an old maid," Heather says. She's an attractive, likeable brunette with bright blue eyes that radiate intelligence, warmth, vulnerability. Her high school yearbook picture is captioned "energetic, witty, fun," she readily relates. But Heather is also Overweight. The capital "O" is at her insistence. More dreaded words are used. The word "fat" had not always been avoided. Her aunts and uncles called her "butterball," and not as a term of derision. The "tyranny of slenderness" was not a phrase she heard in her youth, or even thought about. She grew up in a place where "fat women were not necessarily unloved ladies; they had families, husbands who worked hard," and backyards with kids to go with the rosebushes.

These days, pushing thirty, Heather sees herself edging toward obesity, "the big time." Her heft and weight not only make her feel unfeminine, they convince her that she's alien to men. That's the beauty of being massive, "no one has any interest and I never have to take a chance."

Heather's modifiers are good enough: pretty eyes, self-sustaining, bright, personable, "yet I live a sort of sexless

existence," she says, channeling her passions into historic reno-
vations and rose gardens.

"As a fat person I don't have to deal with rejection. I reject
myself before any man can. When I diet, I find myself inch-
ing towards legitimacy, but whenever I get nervous about it, I
eat my way back into comfortable solitude. It's lonely at times,
but at least I know what to expect. I never have the anxiety of
wondering, Does he love me? I know beforehand, he does not."

* * *

Heather's press trip to upstate New York began at LaGuardia
Airport. The twin-engine 15-seat plane chugged the group to
Albany, then on to Saranac Lake. Of the three men in the group,
Bob Manning was the best looking. "He was a game one, all
right. Spry. Early thirties." A reporter for a suburban St. Louis
weekly, he'd been over-friendly from the get-go ("which got my
suspicions up"), plopping himself down beside Heather at every
opportunity ("bearing down too intently for my liking").

"What did he want? Why was he so aggressive with me? Was
he making fun of me in some way? One of Oprah's 'Men Who
Love Fat Women?' Or a male liberator who has to liberate the
thin woman in me?

"I can't help asking these questions, especially when it's a
Burt Reynolds lookalike. He had to have an ulterior motive." He
had something else; an attractive smile and demeanor she might
have allowed herself to respond to if she looked differently.

While the travel writers went off to visit the Olympic Ski
Jump facility at Whiteface, "I decided to take a skiing lesson."
Sure enough, Bob went along, "so there I was, alone with him
on Mt. Van Hoevenberg."

Outfitted in the latest skiwear, he cut a fine figure while she set off in dowdy dungarees. "I felt inept, trying to finesse my way across the snow, and winding up on my bottom as I slid down the beginner's slope." Bob didn't do much better and they had a good laugh helping each other off the snow again and again.

Late that night, it's just Heather and Bob who wind up in a no-frills upstate saloon, complete with dart board, moose head, and guys in baseball caps. A rifle with a crooked barrel is mounted above the bar; a hand-lettered sign under it reads: "Bill misses bear at 30 feet."

Heather and Bob swill with a will and quickly get bored throwing darts from six feet, so they move further back, letting the darts fly, until the bartender, worried about his liability insurance, angrily insists that they return to the regulation line. They're potted all right; she on Jack Daniels straight, he on the best vodka in the house.

"I was afraid I wouldn't meet anyone after I got divorced," Bob is saying. "I had dates, but I started to think of women as 'the enemy.'"

Heather couldn't help conjuring up images of slim, young girls in running shorts, "girls whose chief claim to fame is their jogging abilities." He told her the gals he'd met in St. Louis since his divorce came in two varieties. "There's the ones in college who are always worried about their finals and what they're gonna do on summer vacation, and the older ones, the ones in their thirties who've been burned so bad they're incapacitated."

In all this he spoke as if she weren't there, as if she were no more than a neutral confidant, a genderless friend who could help him understand.

"The trouble with the babes in St. Louis," was one of Bob's

choice phrases, not only as if she weren't there, or as if she wouldn't be offended by the term "babes," but more importantly, as if these babes were one class of women and she another, as if Bob were sitting with the boys, well, chewing the fat.

When he added, "I need a mature woman," she was ready. Here comes, the bit about needing a woman who is "worn in, ripened, mellowed," preferably not one of these skinny girls who are all hip bones and shoulder blades. He wanted girth, he wanted heft, he wanted heartland heartiness in a gal.

At about two in the morning, when "last call" made the rounds for the handful of people left in the bar, a more inebriated Bob Manning turned to her and said, "Do you ever get lonely, Heather?"

"Why? Do you feel sorry for me?" She knew she sounded too angry, but there you have it. She'd activated the autopilot and the plane was flying itself.

"I feel lonely, that's all," said the man who was not her pilot.

Suddenly the reporter from St. Louis, the one with girl problems back home, suggested that they return to the inn and go to his room. "We can talk," he said. "We won't do anything." She was on her feet, wrapping herself in her massive coat of goose down feathers good to 40 below which is about how cold she felt. Numbed, trembling, she moved toward the door while her mind moved imperceptibly to cornices, window casings, and the thought of renovating the terrace this spring.

On their way back to the inn, he tried to put his arm around her. "I hated the way he made me feel so inadequate. The drunken bastard. He wants to sleep with me and he has the nerve to say, 'I just don't wanna be alone tonight.'"

They walk, beneath a starry sky, without saying a word; at the inn, Heather politely says goodnight. She goes straight to her room and shuts the door. From the other side, Bob Manning says, in a still, sad voice, "Pleasant dreams."

Back in Muncie, at her desk in the newsroom of *The Muncie Star*, on the four to midnight shift, Heather James considers giving Bob Manning a call. He'd talked about going skiing in March and asked if she'd like to come. Instead she taps away at the old Olympia she'd insisted on keeping, fighting off attempts to upgrade her to a word processor, and two hours later she's completed her column for tomorrow's afternoon edition: "Tips on Wainscoting."

Epilogue

Heather James asked us not to reveal the name of the small Midwestern town where she eventually moved to manage the local plant nursery. When she was 44, she married a tree farmer she'd met through work, a "lovely, kind man" in Heather's words. The couple's one big regret is that they were too old to have children. They live in an old Victorian house that Heather has lovingly restored, and they have many close friends. Over the phone, she sounded truly happy.

Kick the Habit

Marjorie Dunne's apartment in Teaneck, New Jersey, is a pleasant shade of blue, the sofa, the carpet, the walls. She's dressed in a snazzy black and white checked suit, red lipstick, blue eyeliner, a string of pearls and large pendant earrings.

She laughs heartily as she sips red wine, pausing to stroke her calico cat, or the tabby that reclines atop the DX7 Moog synthesizer littered with Bach music. She was 66 years old yesterday.

Almost twenty years ago, Sister Marjorie walked through the doors of the Maronite of Holy Cross convent for the last time and emerged Ms. Marjorie Dunne, sweet 47 and never been kissed.

With her Ph.D. in school psychology, the Volkswagen her father had bought her while she was in the convent, and a sum total of $200 for food and clothes, Marjorie Dunne left the cloister that had been her only home for 28 years and lit out into the world never kissed, never touched, never held by a man. She didn't know how to write a check, apply for insurance, or file a tax return. She came out without furniture, clothing, or knowledge of the ways of the world. But she emerged from the convent filled with the rapture of thinking her own thoughts and, for the first time in her life, answering only to herself. The rules had changed, she had changed them!

She was a single, middle-aged woman with lost time to make up for. She had been raised on Staten Island, in a small, clapboard house. Behind the tiny, faded white house, beyond the scrawny plum tree, was a neatly painted, grey and white convent.

The nuns of the St. Louis Academy, in their black habits with the funny white bibs, were friendly to the smart little girl who played alone in the yard. The bright-eyed six-year old knew she wanted to be a nun, and when she was 18, the young woman with a figure that had matured voluptuously, married Jesus.

Her poor, unhappy mother, neglected by Marjorie's philandering father, and desperately clinging to her only child, tried to dissuade her from the life of chastity. "A sexual experience between a man and a woman is the most beautiful thing that can happen to two people," her mother told her. Now Marjorie was determined to have that experience for herself.

A month after leaving the convent, Marjorie landed a job as school psychologist in a Morristown, New Jersey, junior high school. It paid $18,000 a year and she felt rich. She was able to move from her squalid rented room in a North Bergen rooming house to her own apartment. "I was just as happy as I could be."

Her naively honest, optimistic and gutsy approach worked in her favor every time. She told the rental agent at North Bergen's poshest apartment building that she had no money, but she had a job and she could postdate a check. Sure enough, the rental agent allowed it and she moved in.

She needed tires for her battered Volkswagen so she drove over to Sears. She told the guy in the white grease monkey suit, "I just got out of the convent, I have no security of any kind, but I do have a job in Morristown which starts in September. I need tires; can I please have a charge account?"

"Wait a minute," he said and walked off. When he returned, it was with a big smile and a simple declarative sentence that opened a world to her: "Here's your charge account."

She bought everything with it: salt and pepper shakers, plates and silverware, furniture and clothing. Sears card in hand, Marjorie Dunne made a spectacular transformation to civilian life. A friend invited her to a support group of ex-nuns for whom the transition wasn't quite so easy. "But you're much too healthy and happy, you don't belong here," her friend told her.

As she found her stride, her natural good looks blossomed. The former nun bought a white satin negligee in anticipation of... she wasn't quite sure what.

Several months after she began her job at the junior high school, she met a psychoanalyst named Dan Riddle, at a psychology conference in northern New Jersey.

"We talked and had drinks and he invited me to his hotel room. Very interesting man and terribly handsome... tall, bearded and bright, but I declined to go to his room. The next day we got together and we talked the whole day. We talked about sexual experiences and I told him I had been a nun. This got him real excited.

"Come to my room and let's just talk," he said. "Now I knew he didn't want to 'just talk.' I was scared out of my wits but I went anyway." Excited and afraid, she followed him to his room and sat down on the bed. The room was dark and she could hear nothing but the sound of the AirCool working away in the far corner, gently stirring the drapes.

Dr. Riddle sat behind her and put his hands on her shoulders as he talked quietly. Ever so gently, one hand slid along her neck, played with the collar of her blouse, and traced her collarbone. She felt a rush of pleasure and terror; her breathing came too fast.

My God, she thought, I'm going to hyperventilate or worse yet, faint.

"You're so uptight, Marjorie. There's nothing to be afraid of," said Dan. "Why don't you let me give you a massage? It'll relax you. Just lie down here on your stomach... thatta girl. I'll be back in a flash."

She was so innocent, she'd never even had a back rub in her life, but lie down she did, telling herself to seize the opportunity.

He disappeared into the bathroom for a moment and came back buck naked.

"Well, I almost fainted," Marjorie says, recalling that first rush. "I had never seen a man naked before. And he came over to the bed and he just pulled my panty girdle down. Well, I started to tremble, I had an absolute anxiety attack, I was in shock. I could not stop shaking. My teeth were chattering. And I told him, I'm scared to death and I'm just not ready."

"Okay, Marjorie, no rush. Let me just get dressed."

He could not have done or uttered anything more endearing to her. He's not going to hurt me, she thought. I'm not ready, no problem. They lay quietly on the bed, touching hands, and nothing more happened.

Round Two came a few days later when Dan's dog was lost, and Marjorie drove over to his house in Tenafly to help him find it. A torrential rain was falling, and she feared for the dog, but when she got to Dan's house, there was Patches, barking up a storm of his own.

Dan turned to Marjorie, who was standing soaking wet in the doorway. "I know what this looks like."

She laughed and said, "Yes, it really does."

"I didn't make it up," said Dan. "He was really lost. My neighbor must have found him, or else he just came back, right boy? Thatta boy! Won't you come in, Marjorie? Have some tea? Dry off?"

"Well, I don't know."

"Why would I resort to a subterfuge?" he asked. "I'll tell you straight out, Marjorie, I find you very sexy and alluring."

She was blushing. She hovered in the doorway, as paralyzed and afraid as she had been a few days earlier on his hotel bed. She tried to push herself forward through the threshold, but she held back. She would have liked to go in, but didn't know how. She was close enough to smell his damp skin, aware that his body odor aroused strong, unfamiliar sensations in her. She felt drawn up into his power, his aura enveloping, soothing yet frightening her. Was this a power of which the Superiors knew nothing, or did they know it too well, retreating from it in terror? No wonder sex was taboo, it was too powerful to control! To live without it, you had to condemn it first. However much she was falling under his spell, she retreated from his advances. And drove off in the pouring rain.

As she drove home in the downpour, she realized that whatever her struggles in the convent, they weren't like this. As far as sex, sister, you're on your own... no dogma, no Vatican II, no rote catechism. The rain turned to sleet and splattered against the road; the wind picked the water up and flung it every which way, and the storm worsened as she inched ahead in her green Volkswagen.

Over the next few weeks, Marjorie and Dan's friendship grew. They talked often on the phone and saw each other at professional gatherings. She'd grown to like and trust him, felt comfortable with him. The precursors were in place; she was ready to make love to him.

One afternoon, as she was sipping lemonade on Dan's back porch, he crossed his strong arms around her from behind and pulled her in. They kissed in a way that left her defenseless. He had simply taken her by surprise, and she experienced the rapture of surrendering to her feelings.

He was very tender and gentle, and his combination of strength and patience put her over the top in a way she will never forget. There was nothing that could have prepared the ex-nun for the frenzy of happiness she felt on that warm afternoon.

She discovered a sensual being that had remained intact, though buried, all those convent years. As it flowered, a world of ecstatic physical pleasure and delight in the body opened to Marjorie Dunne. As it emerged, she understood the church's biggest lie: the separation between body and spirit, between truth and flesh. She knew there was no more destructive deceit in the church than the cordoning off of sexuality from spirituality, when in fact they were part of the same thing, and everyone had to make their own decisions about both. She began to believe that the essence of health was a rich sex life along with confidence in the sanctity of one's own deepest being.

How many years and struggles it had taken her to liberate herself! She was grateful that she had avoided the fate that met the older nuns, the ones she used to observe with horror who were like walking vegetables, dusting the pews, sweeping the floors and slowly fading away.

Dan was 57 when they met. He and Marjorie saw each other once or twice a week for two years. They always had terrific sex. He introduced Marjorie to lots of interesting people. She enjoyed his company and found him fascinating to talk to, but she did not feel at all possessive about him, and she did not consider making a commitment to him. Once he had proposed to her, and she turned him down.

"Maybe if I'd been desperate. But it would have been a total loss for me. After living under a vow of obedience for 28 years, I wasn't about to toss away my freedom so lightly."

And it's a good thing Marjorie didn't marry Dan. As it turned out, he was a skirt chaser just like her dad. It came as no surprise to Marjorie when he suddenly lost interest in the former nun and announced, "I met the most wonderful Russian princess and I'm going out with her." With surprisingly little regret, Marjorie said goodbye to the man who ended her virginity.

"I learned something important from Dan," Marjorie recalls. "I will always remember him for making my first sexual experience so wonderful that it allowed me to be able to enjoy it again with somebody else."

* * *

In the early 1970s, Marjorie Dunne, nun no more, was something of a swinging single. She went to Club Med and she placed personal ads in the Village Voice. She met men in bars, in restaurants, and at singles clubs. She attributes much of her success to her lucky frou frou, a little black hat she wore whenever she wanted to meet someone new. She went out with many men over the next ten years, and she had four or five serious relationships. Once or twice, she wanted to make a permanent commitment, but it just wasn't in the cards.

In her 40s and 50s, Marjorie experienced all the joys and sorrows that come with the territories of love and sex... unrequited love, broken promises, possessiveness, heartache. Yet she would not change one minute of her life since she left the convent.

By 1980, Marjorie Dunne settled into a quieter life, her "wild oats" having at last been sown. She's one of the few people you tend to believe when she says she loves to be alone. She calls her friends "exceptional" and they number one or two lovers, as well as women both married and single with whom she enjoys a confiding closeness. "They respect my need for privacy and I respect theirs. I enjoy myself."

Marjorie is oblivious to the stigma many people feel about being and doing things alone. Last Christmas she took one of her solo holidays, driving up to Newport, Rhode Island.

"Being a school psychologist can be very taxing, and heart-breaking. A few weeks ago we had a teenager commit suicide and tragedies happen. My work is very stressful and my biggest luxury is to just get away."

In Newport she found a lovely bed and breakfast where she spent Christmas and New Year's. The innkeeper, who she'd spoken to before she left Teaneck, put out a nice bottle of wine for her, along with cheese and crackers, the little wheat ones she loves. When she arrived late that night she enjoyed a light repast in front of the fire before going to bed. She wasn't the least bit lonely despite the other guests being all couples. She ate in restaurants alone, sat by the ocean, climbed over the rocks and did her Christmas shopping in stores that remained open over the holidays. She never once felt awkward or out of place. She is in good health and she feels grateful.

Her friend Alise wanted to join her for the trip, but was politely but firmly turned down. "Sorry, Alise, I really prefer to do this on my own."

Marjorie Dunne is single in America, but it's her own version of single, a rich, full-bodied life that now, from the vantage of her 66 years and counting, appears to lack nothing. But she doesn't whitewash her experience. The convent offered her many opportunities and even when it got in her way, she dealt with the negatives by assuming the responsibility for having chosen to live that way. When she could bear it no longer, she left. But she does acknowledge its legacy both good and bad.

"One of the scars I carry, it's a scar in one way and it's good in another way. I'm able to be alone and I'm happy to be alone; but I think it's also a negative because human beings are social beings and I think that in one way the reason I am happy being alone or want to be alone and don't want to be with somebody else is because I was alone in a crowd for so many years. Twenty-eight years. And I guess, maybe I don't have the courage, or the patience at this age, I don't want to start getting used to somebody else, so it could be selfishness at this point...

"I have no desire to have someone permanent in my life but it could be a hangover of my convent years." On the other hand, maybe it's because, when she's with a man, she tends to put his needs and desires first. "I don't want to create a conflict by saying, 'No, I don't want to do that, I want to do something else,' so I do what they want to do, figuring I'll be alone soon enough. Then I'll do what I want to do."

Epilogue

Marjorie's unusual story grabbed us. If she's alive, she's in her 90s now. We wish we could have gotten her 26-year update. We can only imagine what happened to her.

IV. SCENES & STEREOTYPES

"Very, very vain, my weary search to find
That bliss which only centers in the mind."
Oliver Goldsmith, *The Traveler*

New York City in 1989. Subway tokens cost $1. The real estate market is soft. Fifty-three percent of Manhattan residences are single-person households.

Ed Koch finishes his third and last term as mayor. David Dinkins becomes the city's first black mayor. The homeless crisis has grown to phenomenal proportions. The use of crack is rampant. No part of the city is free of the homeless men and women and the addicts who live on park benches, in subway stations, in door jambs.

Nineteen eighty nine is the year of the Big Comeback for old rock bands from the 1960s and 70s. The Who, the Rolling Stones and Ringo Starr all play the Big Apple.

Black is still the predominant fashion color. Hoop earrings are big. The casual look consists of tight, spandex bicycle shorts and oversized t-shirts or sweaters. Skirts are just above the knee. Western boots make a return appearance.

Leona Helmsley, the "queen of a hotel empire," is found guilty of evading her federal income taxes. New York developer Donald Trump buys the Eastern Shuttle. John F. Kennedy Jr. graduates from NYU law school and is appointed assistant D.A. for Manhattan. The Times Square Redevelopment Project is mandated to preserve the sizzle, the honky-tonk atmosphere, the neon brightness of the Crossroads of America.

Spike Lee, a young film director from Brooklyn, releases a film about racial tensions called "Do the Right Thing." No sooner is the film released when in real life, in Bensonhurst, Brooklyn, a gang of white youths murder a 16-year old black named Yusuf Hawkins.

Protests by environmentalists mount over the proposed permanent docking of a nuclear submarine in Staten Island, while the city launches jail barges on the East and Hudson Rivers to handle the overflow of prisoners.

In spite of the onslaught of pandemonium constantly reported in the headlines, millions find New York irresistible. To many it represents the best, most avant-garde and open-minded place to be for art, music, theater, ideas, dance, and fashion. New York is bursting with opportunities to find success, to find love... if you're lucky.

The singles scene is alive and well, and constantly shifting. Newspaper ads remind us that "beautiful single women do not go to bars," but don't tell the women in Iguana's or Café Society or the hundreds of nightclubs crammed into Manhattan's 20 square miles.

The more jaded New Yorkers only go to a new club on opening night. After that, it's already over, strictly passé. The gay bar scene is lively down around Christopher Street, spilling over to nearby piers on the Hudson River in the summer. On weekend nights, the South Street Seaport is a singles mecca for the Bridge and Tunnel crowd (anyone from New Jersey or a borough other than Manhattan).

For singles intent on being single no longer, frenzied feeding and mating rituals are everywhere. Take Park Avenue South. Any night of the week. Trendy restaurants and bars with thousands of square feet of commercial space and $40,000 a month rents. By nightfall legions of office workers, working women from the outer boroughs, desktop cowboys and suitable suits drift in, liquor flowing and music blowing away the nine-to-five din.

These singles draw their strength in numbers not solitude. In personal interviews, they reveal themselves, but not tonight, not here. Tonight it's superficial surfaces, the exteriors with all the polish. New York, New York.

Lust on the Loose

Brian, Burt and Daryl, the Shearson Lehman brothers, ride into town on their American Express gold cards. Their tab at Canastels at 19th and Park Avenue South will be $178.23 without tip. Their overpriced entrees come with an Odalisque for a waitress, in the sort of mandatory mini with the kind of legs Daryl lives for. Qualifications to work here are major good looks slash aspirations in theater and film.

Like the waitress's legs, the drinks go on forever and with each drink, confidence and the willingness to make a fool of oneself soar. The boys feel good, the boundaries are blurring. Their male hormones walk to the beat of the same drummer, and a Distressing Damsel could lead these Wall Street Galahads anywhere.

Riding the flush of first drinks, they're the masters of the cold call and the leer, the lascivious eye, the hungry heart. During the day they worry about "positions" and "market makers." Tonight they reach into that churning, primordial sludge, "hoping only to get laid," Daryl says. Between sex and money is that vast empty pit into which they toss their drinks.

Daryl, a handsome 38-year-old refugee from Savannah, Georgia, and two broken marriages, sizes up the waitress like a true ladies' man. "You think she'll let me lower her income and raise her taxes?" It's an inside joke for future inside traders.

"Your loss is my commission," Burt sniggers. As a married man just shy of forty, Burt's trip to Canastels is a brothel to the eyes; he can look but not touch.

"Buy junk bonds," says Brian, a weekend sailor who at 27 has decided to tack into the wind of stocks and bonds. "Girls sense my power," he says with deadpan humor. The night before, he and the boys visited Pete's Tavern with a couple of the secretaries and, when Tina, the cutest in the bunch, dallied in the ladies' room, Brian uttered, "She's taking a long time inserting her diaphragm." And he did get lucky that night, but not with her.

A similar pattern unfolds tonight: Brian has the way about him, Burt's hands are tied, and Daryl is intent on making clumsy passes.

Daryl, already a bit drunk, claims to like being single, especially when he contemplates the idea of a red Porsche with a lady in red beside him. "I've always been single at heart," he says, "even when I was married." But it's hard to be entirely persuaded by this good-looking southern boy. "I don't want kids, I want investment vehicles," he says.

Burt plays the fantasy game. It's the old line about being on a diet but looking at the menu anyway. He surveys the pleasure palace with slack-jawed desire, like a man who can't eat the entrees.

Meanwhile Brian has his sights on an Asian waitress. "She's doing a number on my limbic brain."

Brian, Burt and Daryl laugh like cowpokes around the campfire in their leather chaps and spurs after a hard day's roundup. In class each day, Wall Street prepares the three budding stock brokers for rejection. The opening line has to be the clincher or it's strictly "no sale." Like here. Grab their attention right off. Or kiss them goodbye. In Canastels they trade effective openers.

"Mr. Jones, what does the phrase 'financial security' mean to you? Mr. Jones, are you there?"

"Look out your window, Mr. Jones. Do you see the ruffians in the Cadillac? Now, maybe you'd like to reconsider CDs?"

"I can have one of our mobile sales units there in ten minutes, Mr. Jones. With or without the body bag."

Study the cold caller in his natural habitat. Daryl slips his arm around the slim waist of the waitress as she waits for his order. Brian and Burt are embarrassed. Not because he's hitting on her, but because he's botching it.

Slurring his words from the booze, Daryl asks the long awaited question, "What's your name, honey?"

Her eyes roll as she says, "Marie."

"Marie, we're new in town," Daryl says, using his false confiding tone. "Can you recommend a bar where there's some action?"

"Rawhide on Sixth," she declares. They guess, from the name, it's a gay bar. Not a bad joke, either.

"Why don't you join us?" asks Daryl, not noticing what everyone else does. Burt and Brian wince. Come on, man. Get your act together. This is a nice girl. Why would she want a slob like you?

* * *

The following night it's the same. Another day of cold calls, another night at Canastels. Brian scores, Burt fumes, and Daryl, well...

After finishing his Eggplant Canastels, Daryl is pouting. Pouring down the scotches, he reflects that he's been "three months without getting laid! All I do is watch Midnight Blue. Ads for escort services. Phone sex. Blah blah."

The old smooching champeen of Savannah, Georgia, can't make love to a cathode ray tube, now can he?

Marie, the waitress, so all-important last night, is forgotten. Or was that earlier tonight? He doesn't know. But he's replaced her with the "ten" standing at the corner of the bar across from him. "She's incredible," he says, bewitched, bothered and bewildered. Just as he is every five minutes.

"She's doing a valiant job trying to ignore you," says Burt.

"She sees me," says Daryl, loudly enough for her to hear.

Burt orders another round of drinks.

"I can't take my eyes off her," Daryl says.

"Maybe you should have your optic nerve checked."

His ten isn't alone. She's love-cooing with a man in a tailored Italian suit. "What's she see in him?" Daryl wants to know.

"Style, good taste, class," says Brian.

In compliance class today they were asked, "What if you make your pitch and the guy on the other end says, 'Do you own the stock?' What do you tell him?"

"Tell him the truth," says Burt. "If you have a position in the company, tell him. If you don't, tell him anyway." Burt's laugh draws a smile from the leggy waitress. Just his luck, she seems more interested in him than in Brian or Daryl. Being married is a goddamn curse, but judging from Daryl, so is being single.

"Tell him anything you have to, to close the sale," says Brian.

"Exactly. So what do I tell sleeping beauty? I'm her prince?" Daryl nods in her direction, wanting her to see.

"More like the frog," says Burt.

"Tell her, 'Love is never having to say you're sorry when you sit on my face.'"

* * *

After dinner, the boys mosey over to Iguana's, a trendy space with a giant, spangled iguana suspended over the drinking zone, where the ladies press up against them with lusty bodies.

The grueling day of cold calling still plays out in the boys' chopped dialogue.

"The Dun and Bradstreet list sucked, those guys had all been called ten times!" Daryl complains.

"I had a Cortland directory," says Burt sourly.

"In 260? He had 57 call backs," Brian notes, tacking upwind.

"Of those, 13 were maybes," says Burt.

"One of 'em came through," Brian replies.

"I bet he doesn't close the sale. He's not dealing stocks and bonds. Commodities and futures, gimme a break," Daryl whines. He does better when he smiles and says nothing. He drowns his loneliness in scotch and soda. His massive Rolex glares belligerently from his wrist as he lifts his poison from the bar.

Brian's doing better. His Monty Python humor — he knows their routines by heart — wins instant converts-in-skirts.

Roiling in liquor and horniness, Daryl may be good-looking, he may even be smooth on the stock and bond scene, but he needs a new approach here. He's been out of action too long. Things have changed. While he was married, the rules of courtship shifted and he doesn't know them.

Across the bar, I-Wish-I-Wasn't-Married-Tonight smiles a bit too radiantly at a tall blonde. Burt eyeballs her without dissimulation. She doesn't seem to mind being the subject of his market research. She looks amused as he skates over confidently without knowing he's on thin ice.

In her early twenties, with a build like a centerfold, she rattles on about her horse Jared. "He's huge, 16.4 hands. Clydesdales are usually 16.9 so you know he's damn big for a trotter. Got him for a song when Roosevelt Raceway closed," she says.

How quickly those early advances get sticky! She prattles on, as if he's not even there: "He's real spunky, I haven't gotten on his back yet."

"I can trot, I can run, I can do it all," Daryl says to the air.

"Jared's never been in the country before. He's been cooped up all these years."

"Tell me about it," he adds.

"Jared runs and bounds over everything," she says.

To the glue factory with horses named Jared!

"He's so used to going to the finish line, he doesn't know what to do in an open field," she says.

"I'm a strong finisher and I know what to do in an open field." Did he say it, or merely want to say it? Either way, he looks about ready to retire for the night with a cold shower.

"I'm putting in a lot of time with Jared," she continues, obsessed with her quadruped. "He needs a lot of ring work to calm him down. No one's ever ridden him before."

"I'm a thoroughbred," Burt whispers, "and I've been ridden before."

"My friend's a horse trainer, he's got a ring and a barn and everything," she continues. "He used to be my boyfriend but he's married now," she adds.

Burt's not interested in her boyfriend or her horse. By now he can't even remember her name. Was it Jared?

* * *

Scenes like this are repeated not just in Canastels and Iguana's across the street but in big city bars all over the country. It's easy enough to be dismissive about the Brians, Burts and Daryls of the world, but behind their brusque antics is an ardent desire that is more than lust. Isolate them from the madding crowd and each other and they may confide their deeper feelings. Sex may even become a metaphor for union, for not having to be one alone against the world.

"In like wind, out like water." Omar Khayyam wouldn't have given New York's stylish party animals much hope of finding whatever it is they seek in places where they're as hidden from themselves as from others.

Epilogue

Daryl founded a hedge fund in Baltimore, and married for the third time. He has three kids of his own and two stepchildren, a beautiful home with marina access on the Chesapeake Bay and a vacation home in the Florida Panhandle.

Burt divorced, remarried, then divorced and remarried his first wife and mother of his children. They divorced again shortly thereafter, and he remarried for what he avows will be "the last time." Today Burt has been happily re-remarried for almost 15 years in upstate New York, where he is a wealth manager for an investment bank, plays golf and tennis regularly, gives philosophical talks and has two daughters, a stepdaughter and a stepson making their way in the world.

We could not locate Brian.

V. OHIO LIFE

"Every spirit makes its house."
Ralph Waldo Emerson

Family Planning

Southern Ohio in 1971. Mark Williams was eight years old when his father gave him two rabbits which he bred and quickly turned into 170 rabbits. He says this was his first money-making venture. He sold the rabbits, live or dressed, and he bought a brand new 10-speed bike with the proceeds.

He kept the bunnies in pens in the barn, and all was well until a weasel got wind of the arrangement and started making nightly raids on the inventory. One night Mark, armed with his 22-rifle and befriended by his collie named Daisy, spent the night in the barn, determined to peg the weasel before it devoured another gourmet meal.

As you'd expect, a boy of eight can't stay awake all night. Mark fell asleep in the hay bales and when he awoke, he found the weasel dead on the barn's floor. His companion Daisy had taken care of the grisly business while her master slept. Mark still gets choked up today when he relates this story, which could be straight out of an episode of "Lassie" (except for the dead bunnies!).

Imagine Lassie's friend Timmy grown up, 25 years old; that's Mark Williams. Mark had the sort of upbringing Norman Rockwell painted pictures of, and he wants just that sort of life for his adult self, for his family-to-be. He has lived in Ohio all his life, and three years ago a job offer straight out of college brought him to Columbus, the capital of the Buckeye State.

Sitting smack in the center of the state, Columbus is not easy to put a finger on. The highway approaching it is surrounded by fields of corn and soybean. At truck stops, books about Mennonite teenagers and Living by the Word fill the paperback carousels. And then, Columbus with its modest, desultory skyline appears. A city official once said, "Columbus is perceived as 250,000 people who came to the state fair and decided to stay."

The population is double that now, and growing. In February 1989, *Newsweek* dubbed Columbus one of "America's Hot Cities," a city with "jobs, cheap houses and good fishing minutes from downtown."

Four rivers flow through Columbus toward the Ohio. One of them, the Olentangy, flows through the city center, providing good fishing and a nice setting for office workers to have lunch. As the seat of Ohio government, downtown Columbus bustles during office hours, but is quiet at night when everyone retreats to their homes in one of countless subdivisions springing from the corn fields fast as you can say aluminum siding.

Columbus is home to Ohio State University, Jack Nicklaus, the PGA Memorial tournament, and the Columbus Clippers, the Yankees' Triple AAA team managed by Bucky Dent. Mark says it's a town that, "would give anything for a professional sports team. Cleveland and Cincinnati both have professional teams, and it splits Columbus in half. I mean, Browns fans will barely speak to Bengals fans during football season."

Columbus has almost no heavy industry, not a smokestack in sight. The jobs are in the finance, technology, light manufacturing and service industries, and government. Several Fortune 500 corporations are headquartered there. A fair bit of old money is ensconced in large, stone houses in Upper Arlington, but the overall feeling of Columbus is one of middle class incomes and young families.

The expanding city with the small-town feel has been the test market for hundreds of new products. To marketing strategists, citizens of Columbus are the quintessential American consumers. People who live here say it's clean, affordable, safe and a great place to raise a family. But what about being single in Columbus? It suits Mark Williams just fine. Because he was raised on a farm, Columbus is a virtual metropolis for him.

"I like it," he says. "It's a fun town. There's a lot of young, single people. You've got your choice... there's college bars. In the northwest district, it's more of a white collar, young crowd and then if you want to go shoot pool and just hangout, there's pool halls. I'm from a smaller town where everyone went to one type of place, or they didn't go."

Mark has the wholesome good looks and personality which easily win him friends, no matter which bar he goes to. He's a big man, 6'3" and well built, blue eyed, and blond. His pleasant looking face tends to chubbiness around the jaw line, and is disarmingly boyish even with the mustache. He wears dress jeans and a crisp cotton shirt and smells faintly of jasmine soap. When he talks to you, he looks interested and calls you by your name frequently.

Mark would have to be described as All-American. He got his first horse when he was four and his first trail bike at six. He loves to fish and hunt. He speaks very fondly of his youth, his parents and his sister. A studio photograph of his family adorns the bedroom wall of the duplex apartment he shares with a childhood friend. There are other framed photos on the wall: group shots of his ATO fraternity brothers, himself performing at the White House with his high school choir, an aerial shot of the freight terminal where he works.

You would expect to see a 5 X 7 glossy of the All-American girl propped on his dresser to complete the picture, but there isn't one. Even though he's taken out many young ladies in Columbus, Mark doesn't have a steady girlfriend for the time being, but he does have a plan.

"I figure two years in the sales department and I would just assume be single through that, and then possibly move into one of the positions that I feel would be right for me, and at that point, yeah, I would kinda like to get married. And I'd like to have kids, a couple of kids. I'm the last male Williams to carry on my name, and I'd definitely like to have a couple of sons and the traditional, conventional family.

"I'm 25 and I would like to be married before I'm 30. By 30 I would like to say, now I'm married, got a house, got a wife; we're gonna plan children. I look at the fact that as they're growing up, I'd like to do things with them and I don't want to be in my 50s when they're 9, you know, die before they're in high school or whatever."

Mark seems remarkably together for a person of 25. He looks and sounds sincere, but one can't help but wonder if he's unconsciously repeating something he's heard so often that he believes it. Mark's speech is very measured and his soliloquies smack just a little of a sales pitch. It's quickly apparent why he's such a good salesman. Mark is the youngest salesman at a large, national trucking company. He's the young dynamo, a natural; he has just the right combination of personality, energy, confidence, uncomplicated ambition, and discipline to be a good

salesman. He started with The Trucking Company in the oper-
ations department and is climbing the proverbial ladder lickety
split.

* * *

This morning he reports to work at 7:30, and an hour later pulls
out of the parking lot in his new Pontiac Bonneville, complete
with car phone and laptop computer. His 9 o'clock appointment
is known around the sales department as The Bitch.

It's Mark's first visit to her and as he enters the office he quickly
sizes up the situation. A tough cookie all right, a large buxom
woman, in her 40s, with a commanding presence and stern
face. On her desk are photos of some kids and a photo of herself
standing by a deep sea fishing boat, holding a prize-winning
blue marlin.

Mark greets her warmly, like he couldn't wait to meet her,
like he's delighted to have been assigned to her account. He
reaches over her desk, a broad smile on his face, and shakes her
hand with just the right amount of pressure. He seems to be
absolutely enthralled by her business.

"Tell me more about your business, Mrs. Kruger. What lanes
does your freight flow in? What service standards do you have?
Yes, I see. Now what about your special needs? Tell me how The
Trucking Company can service you better."

He sees her face relax as he talks to her... a good sign. She
starts to fluff up her hair with her hand... even better. After 15
minutes, the talk turns from business to chit chat.

"Are those your kids?" Mark asks. "Did you catch that marlin
yourself? Boy, that's a beauty. Do you like to fish?"

He's looking for her "hot button." ("You have to find their hot button. If you're going to entertain, you have to do something they'll really enjoy, to get the most return on your investment. Therefore, you have to read people. I can talk to a guy for half an hour and figure out what he likes, what he wants me to do for him to make him happy. But I have more of a problem reading women.")

Mrs. Kruger and Mark spend 20 minutes swapping fishing stories, laughing, drinking coffee. They set a date next week for an early morning fishing trip on the Olentangy.

Mark stands up to leave and as he's gathering his papers, Mrs. Kruger exclaims, "You know, Mark, I really like your tie. It's such a bold tie."

"Why, thank you Mrs. Kruger."

She gets up, walks around the desk and stands in front of him. "Yes, most men wouldn't wear such a bold tie. It just shows your youth, your outlook."

She's holding the tie by now, examining it closely, her enormous bosom just inches away from his bold tie. Watch out Mark, she's looking for *your* hot button! Ever so subtlety, he pushes his loose-leaf binder an inch or two and it tumbles from the desk to the floor.

"Oh, excuse me," he says, darting to the floor to retrieve it. Then he makes his exit smoothly, "Looking forward to that fishing trip. Now in the meantime, Mrs. Kruger, if there's anything The Trucking Company can do for you, give me a call."

Back at the freight terminal, the guys give him a lot of grief about Mrs. Kruger. "What took you so long, Mark? She's divorced now isn't she?" Yuk, yuk. He takes it in stride. That kind of thing happens to him frequently, and he always handles it tactfully and professionally. Besides, there's one company rule he'd never break: Never get involved, never date a customer.

* * *

When he first came to Columbus, Mark says he, "hit this town hard. I thought I was absolutely rich, first time I ever made money. I'd go out and drop as much as $100 in a night, buying girls drinks, just getting crazy." For the last year though, since he's been working 14-hour days in sales, Mark hasn't had much time for a personal life, but he doesn't really mind. He says he likes his job and sees it as just one stepping stone toward his quest for a happy life.

"I've come to a point now where I feel that I've done what I wanted to do being single. You know, I've sown the wild oats, or whatever. I've run around all night, all weekend. And I'm sure that down the road when I'm married, there's gonna be that feeling again like, whoa I missed that. For now I'm happy being single.

"The way I look at it... I'm single; I have no ties in Columbus, just my apartment. If I can golf with customers and go out to dinner and have lunch and breakfast and go to the racetrack, all this for free, entertain myself and entertain these customers and I don't have anyone to answer to or plan things with... it's better for the company.

"I figure probably two years in sales, and then if everything goes well, there's a position as division field trainer or branch manager. Do that for about three years so they get some return on their investment. But after that, you basically write your own ticket. I'd like to end up some day as a regional manager or division vice president, something like that."

* * *

The citizens of Columbus are wild about golf. How many other towns have a public course designed by Robert Trent Jones? They can't build golf courses fast enough to keep up with the demand. Mark has an 11 o'clock appointment to play nine holes at Hickory Hills. Being in sales has done wonders for his golf game; his handicap is down to 18.

At 2 o'clock, he has a late lunch with the traffic manager of a fertilizer company at a sports bar/restaurant called Rocky's. They'll catch a few innings of the Reds game on TV while they have a couple of beers and discuss business. They both order the Three Alarm Chile and split an order of Champion Potato Skins. Mark's client, Ed, is in his 50s and recently divorced, determined in his middle age to reach for all the gusto he can. Oddly enough, Mark feels partially responsible that so many of his clients are single in America.

"A lot of my customers are men who have hit their second childhoods. It's like they've been married for 18 years, have kids in their teens, and now they're getting divorced and they're running around all the time. And they like hanging out with me. It bums me out because I get paid to do that. But I feel that's one reason these guys are getting divorced. These traffic managers are entertained, I mean top notch entertainment all the time, and they play salesmen from competing companies against each other. And that does upset me a little bit."

Mark arranges to take Ed to a Clippers game the following week. They part, and he returns to the terminal to finish some paperwork. By 6, he's home to grab a quick shower and change of clothes. By 7:30, he's at Scioto Downs waiting for his clients, a married couple who own a clothing company and have a passion for the trotters. He's lucky to get home early tonight, by 9:30. Luckier still, the clients were winning all evening.

"It's always best when the client wins," Mark winks.

* * *

It's not all work and no play for Mark Williams. He met a girl a month ago when she was his waitress at a business lunch. He likes her a lot and feels "this great desire to be with her as much as possible," but he already suspects it's not for the long run. She's a first year law student, so he figures she'll be building her career just at the time when he wants to start a family. Bad timing. Mark is nothing if not practical and he suffers no romantic illusions about love and marriage.

"I think 'finding the right person' is kind of a euphemism. You're not gonna meet somebody and think oh, my God, I'm in love, let's get married, let's live happily ever after. It's not gonna happen. I think you find someone who's looking for the same type of life, get married, buy a house, and start a family. You have to care about someone and want to be married to them, because you have to work at it like anything else. It's the give/get/merge kind of thing. If that's what you want then you can be happy at it."

Is it unusual for one so young to put practical parameters on love and life the way Mark does so glibly? He is not yet adequately set up to be married, but everything about him suggests that being single is simply a phase. He'll be married by the time he's 30. Ambiguity and doubt don't trouble him. Mark smiles as he sums up his life to date. "So far, I'm pretty much on track with where I want to be."

Epilogue

The authors were delighted to discover that Mark Williams's life — at least the big events in his personal life — turned out pretty much as he'd planned and hoped 26 years ago. At age 25, he did indeed marry the law student mentioned at the end of his story. Mark and his wife have been happily married ever since, and they have two sons who are both in college. He still works as a salesman in the trucking industry, but he postponed his ambition to rise high in the ranks of management in order to spend more time with his sons. He enjoyed being his sons' Cub Scout leader and coaching their baseball, basketball and soccer teams through the years. Displaying the same positive attitude he did in 1989, Mark told us, "It's been a good 25 years and I'm still excited about what the future will bring."

The Doctor's Widow

Charli Pearson is trying to sell her house in Lakewood, Ohio, an affluent suburb of Cleveland. It's been on the market for six weeks and she's starting to get worried. "Even Donald Trump would be worried by now," she quips. "I don't understand it. Houses in the neighborhood put on the market at the same time as mine sold in a snap."

She stands, looking out at a gentle rain, in the front door of a well-kept white colonial with black shutters set in the center of a large, wooded lot on a cul-de-sac. Having just returned from a jazzercise class, she wears white shorts, a navy polo shirt, and aerobics shoes. Charli describes herself as a woman with "a liberal ideology and a conservative lifestyle."

There's a dignity and softness about Charli Pearson, single and alone at 54. She's tall and poised, and she speaks properly, almost formally, but that's countered by her expressive, pliant face and her tendency to giggle. She wears her wavy, blondish hair swept to one side at chin length. Her strongest features are a pair of luminous, doe-like eyes and a toothy smile. She's got a slight overbite you notice when she laughs.

Charli's daughter, Erin, lives in Manhattan on the Lower East Side. She's a striking girl of 25, quiet, intelligent, intense and very observant. She's got the sort of sharp features which photograph well and a shocking head of blond, Rastafarian dreadlocks. She wears a second-hand black dress and hiking boots.

Like her mother, Erin's conversation is generously sprinkled with giggles ranging the scale from deep chortles to high pitched twitters. Neither Charli nor Erin look like gigglers, but there you have it.

Erin says her mother's looks have always reminded her of Mary Tyler Moore. "She's got that same kind of vibrant innocence, and that wonderful smile."

The house, like Charli, is friendly and literary. It holds hundreds of books, neatly aligned in solid, oak bookcases built into the walls. The furniture and style are antique looking, but not stuffy; the house is immaculate, yet comfortable. It has the pleasing, woody smell of dried eucalyptus. A grey Persian sleeps curled up on the pewter blue sofa under the yellow orb of light cast by a reading lamp. Perched on a high bluff at the edge of Lake Erie, Charli's house has spectacular, panoramic views of the Great Lake which extends as far as the eye can see.

Lakewood is only six miles from downtown Cleveland, yet it feels like a small town. Not a suburb, but a town in its own right. In the board game Trivial Pursuit, Lakewood is mentioned twice: once as the safest city in America, and the second time as the American city with the highest percentage of homosexuals after San Francisco. Residential streets are shaded by huge, old maple trees, and lined by multi-story wooden houses with dormer windows. Houses painted in pastel colors with contrasting bric-a-brac trim. Houses with front-porch swings and rose trellises. American flags wave from the lampposts, and toddlers on tricycles pedal furiously along the sidewalks while their mothers lean over fences and chat with neighbors.

Erin grew up in Lakewood and didn't like the town much, but she comes home regularly, as she has now, to visit her mother. The Lake and the beach are its only redeeming qualities in her opinion. She left for New York as soon as she was old enough. She says that underneath the quaint look of the town is a strange, seething quality.

"Lakewood is actually full of inbred freaks, weird families," Erin explains. "Oh, the houses seem all right on the outside, but you go in and there's no furniture. In one house I was recently in, there was an old guy with arthritis sitting in the dark watching a hockey game, totally oblivious to us. In another, this 28-year-old kid lives upstairs with total control over his parents. Smoking pot and listening to heavy metal music all day. His mother never changes out of her bathrobe. It's so depressing."

Some of the houses near the Lake are veritable mansions, built 60 or 70 years ago as summer cottages for Cleveland's elite. There are French chateaux, English castles and Southern plantation manor houses, each set deep back on expansive lawns fronting the wide, tree-lined boulevard. What really goes on behind the walls of those mansions?

"As a kid, I used to walk dogs for those wealthy eccentrics," Erin says. "I'll tell you what you'll find in those beautiful mansions... you'll find two old women, living in their kitchen, with linoleum floors and tin cabinets. They sit all day and watch soap operas on black and white TVs. In another, there was a drunk old man with a bloody nose all the time, who sat in a room full of cigar smoke. It's not that they don't have money, it's just that they're just... gone.

"Black guys do their lawns and the places look great from the outside. Inside, some of them have no furniture anywhere, and dog shit all over. Not really what you'd expect. It's sort of strange southern gothic."

"Oh Erin, you *do* see things from an interesting slant," Charli says, amused as all get out by her daughter's view of the world.

Charli has lived in her house for 25 years. She raised her family in it, and has been there alone for the past eight years since her husband, a physician, died of heart failure. Now, she's making a fresh start. She recently bought a condominium in a younger, more liberal section of town where she plans to move once her house is sold. She says she could never leave Lakewood.

"There's a hokey, small-town feeling in Lakewood that I like," Charli explains as she sips iced tea on her back porch. "You know, on the Fourth of July they put out flags, and there are concerts in the band shell in the park on Sunday nights. I like that small town flavor a lot. It doesn't seem like Cleveland. My children tease me about Lakewood, about my provincialism," she chuckles.

"Yes, it's a small town all right, but it's also very prejudiced," Erin comments. "The police used to say on the radio something like, 'Nil spotted between 3rd and 4th.' It stood for 'nigger in Lakewood.' You know, cops would harass my black friends for broken brake lights and stuff. Black people were only good for mowing the lawns for rich white women. I found it pretty stifling here. "

* * *

Mother and daughter are seated on wicker furniture covered in pale blue and yellow cushions on Charli's screened-in back porch, facing Lake Erie far below. A misty, veil-like rain, what Ohioans call a "farmer's rain," is falling. The weather has painted the Lake and the sky the same shade of grey, making it impossible to tell where one blends into the other at the horizon. The effect is calming. A few sailboats, quite small in the distance, tack through the water in spite of the rain.

"Being married to a physician more or less prepared me for widowhood," Charli begins. "I spent a lot of time alone. Because my husband was successful, he was always at the hospital or seeing patients, or tired or sleeping.

"The thing about being widowed — and I hate the word, it's such an ugly word — the thing about being widowed is there's some dignity to it. For my friends who are divorced, it can be horrible, ongoing. At least for me, it's final."

Erin remembers her father as a great doctor whose patients adored him. He was attractive, intelligent, charming and took time with each patient. When she worked one summer as his receptionist, she was terribly proud of him. She says he was highly disciplined and allowed no excess in his life. From reading the books he used to read, she's discovered he was an existentialist. Erin believes that as he grew more disappointed in life, he took it out on his family. During his last few years, he was sick with diabetes and deeply depressed.

Charli says she was happy in her marriage, 90 percent of the time. The last 10 percent, when her husband got sick and spent all his time alone in the study, weren't so good.

"Yes, they always seemed happy to me," Erin observes. "You know, they were doing what they wanted to do... two kids, two cars, little vacations to Williamsburg. They were similar. They even looked alike. They socialized with the crowd, but they were light about it. They didn't get involved in any of the crap."

"Do you really think we looked alike?" Charli asks as she returns to the porch from the kitchen and places a plate of warm, sliced banana bread on the glass topped coffee table. She sits perfectly still and watches the lake for a few moments before speaking again. She and Erin both know how to plant themselves in a chair and sit without moving. Neither of them fidgets, nor gestures with her hands. All the movements and expressions are in their faces. Charli has a crisp voice and she enunciates every word carefully, precisely.

"The worst thing that ever happened to me was my husband's death," she reflects. "I was holding his hand in the hospital when he died suddenly of a seizure. Once you survive something as awful as that, anything that happens after that is… nothing.

"But I think out of everything bad, something good comes. My husband's death made me stronger. I mean I wouldn't wish him to die for me to be stronger, but that's what happened. I'm more independent now in thinking for myself. And it made my children and me much closer. The three of us just clung together. That was nice."

"My Mom wasn't much of a personality before he died," Erin says slowly. She has a low, quiet voice and a way of tensing her face around the eyes as she concentrates on what she's saying. "She played tennis, was a mother, did substitute teaching, always read a lot. It was the best thing in the world for her when he died; she started to know herself."

"Yes, but it was very hard that first year," Charli responds. "I look back and don't know what I did. I think I was in a state of shock for a while.

"Being alone in Cleveland… Cleveland is a very couple-oriented city. It's divided, the east and west, divided by bridges and this river. The east side is more liberal, democratic, free thinking, and the west side, over here, is very conservative and couple-oriented. So the first year after my husband died, I was invited places by our old friends, but gradually the invitations from couples fell off. I don't really know why, maybe I was a reminder of what could happen to them."

"Mom took up jazzercise!" They chuckle.

"My children tease me in my 'cute' leotards, but jazzercise was my panacea after my husband died. You see, I don't do the bar scene."

"One time Mom and I went out together as single women," Erin says. "And she got drunk after one scotch! She doesn't drink, and if she does, she gets drunk too fast. I couldn't go out with her anymore." She shakes her head, her dreadlocks bobbing from side to side, and they share a smile.

"I tried it a couple times... going to a bar with a divorced friend, and I couldn't stand it. I don't drink and I find the bar scene kind of lonesome. They're crowded, but isn't there a lonesome feeling to it?"

* * *

There's not one man in Charli's life now, but there are many men: William Faulkner, John Cheever, William Styron, John Steinbeck, Nathanial West, and Patrick White. There are women too: Joyce Carol Oates, Joan Didion, Katherine Mansfield, Eudora Welty. Charli's passion is reading and studying literature and authors.

"When she talks about literature is when she gets most clear," Erin confides when her mother's out of the room. "We can really talk then; we share that."

Charli considers a turning point in her life as having occurred two years ago, when she was taking a literature course in a college adult education class. It was during that period she was also seeing a therapist for the first time because she felt an enormous anxiety about the lack of direction in her life. Her children were gone, her husband was dead, she was well set financially and had no pressing need to work, but she was restless. What was the point to her life anymore?

One day after class, Charli approached the course coordinator and asked if she might be given the chance to teach a course. She was told they'd consider her if she'd present a sample course at the upcoming Sampler Day.

For two months, Charli worked on the author, John Cheever. She read everything by and about him she could find. She realized she was terrified of speaking in front of a group, and turned to her therapist, Cindy, to help her overcome that fear. In the end, her presentation on Sampler Day was a great success. She was hired by the school and given free rein to invent and teach courses on the authors she chose. Preparing and teaching those courses has become the center of her existence. She thrives on it, and as a result is one of the school's most popular teachers.

"It's quite something, isn't it! I've found my little niche here. It's what keeps me sane. And you know, what I lack in *knowledge*, I make up for in *enthusiasm*," Charli says, laughing joyfully. She talks on and on, her face rapt, about the authors she loves, about the Faulkner conference she attends every summer in Oxford, Mississippi. She meets quite a few interesting men at those conferences at Old Miss, but none for whom she "feels the right chemistry" for a relationship.

She met a man with the right chemistry in Lakewood two years ago, but the relationship is far from ideal. She's terribly embarrassed when she admits he's 15 years her junior.

"I don't bring him to my friends' dinner parties because I can just imagine them whispering in the kitchen, 'What's Charli doing with that young guy?' Cindy, my therapist, says I'd better evaluate the relationships with my friends, rather than the age difference with him," she snickers.

He had been recently divorced when they met at a Kentucky Derby party. He was working by day and going to law school at night. He's since passed the bar exam.

"It's a very one-sided relationship in that he's so busy, he only sees me when he's free. He's a very disciplined person, and I like that in him, and I like the intelligence. That's what attracted me. We can share things on an intellectual level and that's hard to find.

"But, if I ask him to come over for dinner, it's always 'No, Charli, I have too much work to do.' Yet I'm always there for him. Cindy thinks he's selfish, and she thinks my husband was selfish too. She's trying to work on why I'm attracted to selfish men. Don't you love that?"

Erin, who's been standing in the backyard watching sea gulls overhead, while quietly listening to this conversation about the 'boyfriend,' commented later when her mother was out of earshot.

"I think he's totally wrong. They're obviously on different paths in life. It would be the same trap as she was in before. I think he reminds her of my father. He even looks like him and he's disciplined. I think she needs someone a lot lighter. But... she has very high ideals which I'm glad."

Charli doesn't see the young lawyer all that often, once or twice a month, and they talk on the phone a few times a week.

"He called me three times last week," she says, obviously delighted by that much attention. "We do have a nice time when we go out, and he'll say really nice things to me like 'I appreciate you, Charli.' That's nice, and when he has a problem he'll call me and we'll talk about it. But he's running scared. He's afraid of being hurt. I can see that in him."

"Humph," is all Erin has to say to that. The screen door slams shut behind her as she comes back on the porch and wipes her wet boots on the door mat.

"Erin hasn't met him... but she's very protective of me. Like with Ralph, the man next door. His wife just died last winter. He used to flirt with me when she was alive, but that's just his personality. He's a salesman.

"Recently he's come over and made little like... propositions. And I said one night, 'Oh, Ralph, just because I'm alone and next door, proximity does not a romance make!' I told Erin and she said, 'Oh my god, he looks like Benny Hill! He has no class. He's not your type at all.'"

The memory of this sends them both into a fit of high-pitched giggles.

* * *

Later in the evening, Charli and Erin make the final preparations for dinner. The zucchini casserole baking in the oven is nearly ready. Charli is washing lettuce and Erin is cutting the tomatoes for a salad. The kitchen has a French provincial look, large blue and white square tiles on the floor and copper pots and omelet pans hanging on the wall. A round, rustic wood table matches the cupboards, and a pass-through in the wall opens into the dining room. Several stools are aligned in front of the counter created by the pass-through. Erin is seated on a stool, and Charli is standing by the sink.

"Over the years, my friends have tried to fix me up on blind dates," Charli says as she rotates the handle of a lettuce spinner.

"But who needs that? It would be nice to have a man in my life, but I honestly don't feel that need. And I don't feel that I'm a reject, that I'm inadequate. In many ways I'm very contented with my life right now. I'd be more contented if I could sell my house.

"I'm too independent now maybe. You know... that's a turn off to men. I think men my age like to feel they're needed. They like a woman to be a little more dependent, a woman who will bat her eyelashes and tell him what big shoulders he has. I was never good at that even when I was young... it's so phony. I sometimes think my independence is threatening to them. And men my age want to impress with their jobs, their golf scores, their big cars... it's so boring. They get tired and go to bed so early. By 10 o'clock, this neighborhood is asleep! I'm in a funny place in my life."

"And the only decent ones your age are chasing 20 year olds, right Mom?"

"Yes, Erin, that's the sad truth. Though, I don't really get lonely anymore. I get restless at times, especially in the evenings, around dinner time. I don't know why. But I always have my books. And I play tennis and do my exercise."

"You're never really alone because you have Beatrice!" Erin exclaims. Beatrice is the cat. The two of them laugh because they share the knowledge that Charli dotes on Beatrice who does actually provide some companionship.

Charli says she would never marry again, no benefits in it at her age. She paraphrases something Margaret Mead wrote that she endorses: people need different partners at different stages in their lives, and it's unrealistic to expect people to spend 40 years together because they're bound to grow in different directions.

"You know, when Willard Scott on the Today Show says, 'Congratulations to Mabel and Harold celebrating their 70th wedding anniversary today,' I think, oh those poor people. They've missed so much in life by just looking at each other over the breakfast table every morning. So... that's kind of how I feel about marriage anymore.

"You see, living alone... a certain selfishness has evolved in me, and maybe that's not so bad after years of nurturing and raising a family and thinking of other people's needs before my own."

Charli explains that she used to feel guilty about enjoying being alone, but now she's trying to accept that she's not "so bad." She readily admits that Erin's visits and support of her new-found independence mean the world to her.

"Oh yeah, Mom loves it when I visit," Erin says teasingly, "but you see this stool I'm sitting on? If I spin it wrong, she'll fix it the moment I leave the room. Secretly, she can't wait till I leave, so she can put the house back in order."

"Oh, Erin, I'm not that bad, am I? It's true, I have gotten fanatical about the house, especially since I've been trying to sell it. You never know when a realtor will call and bring some people through."

The only time Charli seems vulnerable and insecure, even frightened, is when she talks about selling her house. She knows it's not rational, but she feels every rejection of her house by a potential buyer is a rejection of her life in the house. People traipse through her house, her life, and whisper comments to the realtor about this or that not being right.

"Oh you feel like you must be living in a sleaze," she moans, "but my realtor tells me some people just can't afford it so they start to knock it. Two weeks ago I just sat here crying. I mean I think I've done the right thing, but when I do sell and I sign that paper, it's going to be hard. I have 25 years in this house.

"And there's really no one to help me with this decision. It's tough. I think maybe I should have sold the house before I bought the condo, but what if I had no place to go. Emotionally, I'm at the condo already. It was a big decision because for a long time, I thought I'd stay here till I died."

Erin is visibly concerned at seeing her mother so upset. Her brows crease over dark, serious eyes focused straight ahead as she thinks of the right thing to say. She stops slicing a cucumber and looks up.

"I think it's a good move, Mom. You should have done it sooner. This house was our childhood, your childhood, and it's not there anymore," she says.

Charli looks lighter, bolstered by Erin's words of encouragement. "Erin, you're right. This condo will be my very first own place, at this late date in my life. No memories, no one telling me where to put the couch. Everything will be mine, and I kind of like that. It's like starting out. Granted most people do it when they're 22! I've just delayed it. Maybe it's good to wait, keeps your enthusiasm high."

Erin adds, "You've outgrown this area really. It died, and people who have died with it can stay here. But you're better off getting out of here."

"It's true. More and more I find myself thinking of something Hemingway once said about Oak Park, 'It was just broad lawns and narrow minds.' And I think, my god, that's where I am.

"Where I'm moving, the condo, now there's an interesting crowd. A lot of gay people and older people, all ages come to think of it. I've met people in the elevator already. I just go over there to think where I'm going to put furniture, how I'm going to arrange my study," Charli reflects.

She's occupied for the next couple of minutes, tossing the salad, taking the casserole out of the oven, perhaps thinking about where she's going to put the desk in her new study. It's quiet in the kitchen except for the soft ticking of a clock and the sound of the rain, still falling steadily at dusk. Erin leaves the room momentarily and returns with Beatrice, who looks uncomfortable in her cradled arms.

"This neighborhood — here's how I remember it from a kid," Erin reflects. "They all started out as young, beautiful people with new money, orange lipstick, hot pants, J&B with a twist, swimming pools and tennis parties. They all had little gourmet shops. Then it started falling apart... they all started disintegrating, having affairs, losing their jobs, admitting they were homosexual."

Charli is very amused, "My god Erin, you grew up in a John Cheever novel! You really are too much."

"A friend once posed a hypothetical question to me. He said, 'Who would you want to be with if you only had two hours to live?' And I didn't even have to think, I just said 'I'd like Erin to be with me.'"

"That's really nice. Thanks, Mom," is all Erin replies as she continues to set the table.

Charli waits a few seconds, anticipating more of a response. "Okay Erin," she says, still waiting. "Now, you're supposed to say you'd want to be with me."

Not one to play into a set up like that, Erin thinks a moment, then replies, "No, Mom, if I had only two hours to live, I'd take some books and a six-pack and go off into the woods and have a grand old farewell party by myself."

Charli laughs joyfully. "Oh that's just perfect," she exclaims. "So typically Erin. Come on, let's eat," as she sets the casserole on the table.

"Say, did you get a chance to read that Robert Penn Warren novel I sent you yet?"

Epilogue

Charli Pearson sold her house and moved into her condo in Lakewood shortly after this interview. She eventually did re-marry, and she outlived her second husband. Charli continued to get great joy out of teaching and discussing literature. She passed away in 2011.

VI. THREE BACHELORS

*"All creatures in the world through love exist,
and lacking love, lack all that may persist."*
Shakespeare, *Much Ado About Nothing*

Love, Who Needs It?

Palm Beach, Florida in July. The sun is relentlessly hot and white as a flash bulb. Clean air bathes the opal-colored sea and emerald green lawns of mansions commanding their private beaches, mansions closed for the summer, left to trusted gardeners' care until owners return next winter for the season. Clusters of palm trees shade the empty dwellings, shuttered closed against the possibility of hurricanes. No one's there to hear the soft thump of mangos and coconuts dropping onto spongy lawns.

It seems unnaturally still, and the slightest disturbance is noticed. A trespasser walking along the high tide line of the deserted beaches draws patrol cars within minutes. They silently comb the exclusive neighborhoods, sensing intruders the way sharks sense blood.

Inland from the beach lies the perfectly manicured Town of Palm Beach. Modern, immaculate, tastefully done in Spanish tiles and Royal Palms, it's a shopping mall for its wealthy taxpayers and guests. Gucci, Van Clef and Arpels, and Saks front Worth Avenue, dubbed "the shortest, richest street in the world." Business is sluggish in July.

Across the intracoastal waterway, lies West Palm Beach's middle class neighborhoods of modest ranch houses with carports, shopping malls containing Sear's and J. C. Penney's, busy stretches of utilitarian highway lined by muffler shops, hardware stores, and coffee shops. It's business as usual here, even in July.

West Palm Beach cooks under the midday sun. Its citizens dart from car to work to shop to house, seeking the cool respite of air conditioning and shady places. They look forward to the weekend when they can go out in their fishing boats on the intracoastal, or to the beach at Lake Worth, or maybe to the Burt Reynold's Dinner Theater for a night out.

Carlo Morante lives in a house badly in need of repair, on a half-acre, corner plot just off a busy, commercial street in West Palm Beach. It's a two-story framed stucco built in 1938, a boxy house the color of sand. His blue van is in the driveway. The yard is shaded by pine, mango, orange and lemon trees. At the end of a long, steel chain tied to a tire under the trees is Carlo's dog, a mixed Doberman/German Shepherd named Duke, a former "Pet of the Week" whom Carlo rescued from the Animal Rescue League.

Carlo lives on the second floor; the first floor is not habitable. The house isn't air conditioned, but it's cool inside. In 1938, they made the walls thick, and the roof's long eaves provide shade. Tin awnings and dusty venetian blinds protect windows exposed to the sun. The floor is bare and the drab furniture is second-hand. Huge portions of drywall have chipped away, leaving the wood framing of the house exposed in much of the living room, and what's left of the interior paint is peeling off.

Strewn about the floor and end tables is Carlo's office equipment: an adding machine, typewriter, floor plans, file cabinet, briefcase, rolodex. He's a general contractor. He builds houses in the Palm Beach area, and he likes his work. Someday soon, he intends to convert the house he's living in into a duplex. He got a great price on the land.

At 31, Carlo lives alone, has never married and says he never wants to marry. His parents are Sicilian, and he has their olive complexion and dark eyes and hair. He's on the short side and solidly built with a face you can read like a boxer's. You can see where his nose was broken more than once, where his head was split open in several places, where his jaw was knocked off center. He's not handsome, but he's masculine, virile looking. Women who've known him say he has animal magnetism. He has the slow, deep, Southern voice of a country western singer.

Getting women to sleep with him has always been a snap, but his friends, long-time buddies from high school, contend he doesn't hold women in very high regard.

* * *

"Carlo thinks all women are whores. All he does is jump 'em. But he's brought home some of the most beautiful, rich women in Palm Beach to that run-down hole he lives in. And they always want to come back to him."

"Carlo picks up chicks real good... he talks good trash."

"I don't think he'd consider marrying a girl who wasn't a virgin. He used to like to knock off virgins."

"Carlo is animalistic... he finds the weakness in someone and goes straight for it."

* * *

"When I talk to a woman and look into her eyes, I can touch on a few different things and tell by her face, and know how I can get to her," Carlo says.

He sits on the sunken cushions of a brownish couch in his living room. A rotary fan on the coffee table stirs the air just a little. He's wearing a sleeveless t-shirt and short shorts, and he's talking about women and the way things are in 1989. He speaks at a controlled, almost monotone level.

"Things are different than they used to be. Standards have changed... mainly because of disease and drugs. I smoke a little pot, I don't drink that much anymore. Just pot, that's the only drug I do. And you've got crack cocaine prevalent everywhere you go.

"I met a girl the other day. We went to a convenience store, me and a friend, he was driving. And I went in the convenience store, and as I came out I saw this real good looking blonde drive by in a car. She parked the car and walked behind the building. So I told my friend to drive behind the building to see where she went cause I knew it was dark back there. I couldn't see why she went there to begin with.

"So we drove back there and she was knocking on this pizza parlor's door yelling. And I just yelled out the front window, 'Hey what are you doing?' She says, 'Well, a friend of mine works here and I'm just stopping by to see him, but I don't think anybody's here.'

"So she had walked up to our car by this time and I could see she'd been drinking. And she was about 20 years old, extremely pretty, driving a brand new Jaguar, dressed real nice, but I could tell she was drinking. So I talked to her about two seconds and I asked her if she'd like to come home with me. I can pick things up in women on the spur of the moment... something told me if I wanted her I could have her right then.

"She goes 'OK.' And I mean this wasn't a tramp, a street walking person. Her dad lived in Palm Beach on the ocean. He was extremely wealthy, but he was under investigation for some bullshit, I don't know what. So she got in the car and said to me 'Do you smoke rock?' I was in the front passenger seat, my friend driving, and the girl in the back seat. And I said, 'No I don't smoke rock, why do you?'

"And she said 'Yeah, are you sure you don't want any?' And she opened up her hand and she had about $500 worth of rocks in her hand. I asked her what she was doing with the rocks, and she says, 'Me and my sister bought it. I haven't been doing it very long, but you get these cravings.'

"And I said, 'Well if you're coming home with me, you have to throw the rock out the window.'

"That's how blunt. I mean that just shows you how standards change. This was a beautiful girl... blonde, 20 years old, clean, and I told her either throw the rock out the window or get out of the car. So the girl was almost crying, and she couldn't do it, so I made her get out of the car and we left her right there.

"Ten years ago, the rock wouldn't have come into play anyway. But I'm just so down on cocaine rock. I've seen too many lives destroyed by it. That prevailed over getting a piece of ass. Something was more on my mind than just getting a piece of ass. I could make the distinction between what I wanted."

Carlo felt good about himself when he left the beautiful blonde in the parking lot, like he'd done the right thing, a feeling he was not all that familiar with. Standards certainly had changed for Carlo Morante, who seven years ago was doing a brisk business as a cocaine dealer, selling it up and down the east coast. He got out of the business when it got too dangerous, when he never left the house without carrying a gun.

He was also housing two prostitutes at the time, one he'd picked up at a bar, not realizing she was a hooker. He let her stay at his house and she brought a friend. They turned tricks and paid Carlo handsomely. He was making money hand over fist and he spent it as quickly, taking his friends out nightly and footing the bills for their good times.

* * *

"Carlo was fun to hang with. He was generous. Things happened when you went out with Carlo. This can be a pretty dull town."

"He was the ringleader in high school, dreaming up outrageous shit. Harmless stuff really, but enough to keep us in trouble."

"Carlo will do anything for you. He's always been a real good friend... but I don't like him."

"He always got in fights when he went out. If you went out with Carlo, you'd best leave early if you didn't want to get involved in a fight."

"He never did anything wrong to me... he's a loyal friend, a real good friend."

"Carlo's the beneficiary of my life insurance policy from work. It's only enough money to bury me, but I can trust him to take care of burying me the way I told him."

* * *

After the drug business folded, Carlo went to Saudi Arabia for a year where he made $1,000 a week cash hanging drywall. He came home and spent money lavishly in the pursuit of pleasure and women, until he ran out of money again. His life consisted of "partying and getting laid." He picked the women up at bars.

"If I go to a bar for the sole purpose of finding a woman, I start at one end of the bar, give a line of bullshit to one woman and, if it doesn't work, just go right on down the line, and sooner or later you're gonna meet somebody who's gonna take the line of bullshit."

He'd rarely sleep with the same woman twice, and felt a particular animosity toward a certain type of woman.

"I don't hate women, well maybe to a degree. If the only thing they're interested in is money. Those women I hate, because they're looking for a meal ticket. I don't feel like being anybody's meal ticket. I don't remember who said it... a man will marry down, but a woman never will. Most women, if you're poorer than they are, they don't want anything to do with you.

"Palm Beach is full of superficial women who try to put on a big front, or they go to bars where they think men with money hang out, so they can snag one... they disgust me. I talked to one girl recently, I walked over and said 'How're you doing?' And I bought her and her girlfriend a drink, and I turned around to talk to her. But she told me she wanted to finish her conversation with her friend. So she turned around eventually to me and the first words out of her mouth were 'What kind of car do you drive?'

"And I told her that I drove a Porsche and I was worth about $30 million. I didn't say it like it was bullshit; I looked her right in the eyes and said this.

"I was lying right to her face, but I wanted to see her reaction. All of a sudden her and her girlfriend's conversation ceased, and I mean now I was interesting. To which point, after one more drink, I said to her 'What the fuck do you drive, honey?' And she told me, and I said 'Well you're a piece of shit, you're a little too below me.' And I left her sitting at the bar stool with her mouth wide open."

* * *

"He's a mean son of a gun. His father was a mafia man, heartless."

"His family, they were all wild. And his Mom was real submissive."

"I've seen Carlo fuck up 5 people, 5 bouncers. Carlo's bad. Kickboxing. He doesn't look like much though, does he? But he can set himself well. He uses the ground. One punch, he can knock somebody out."

"He had his mother wrapped around his little finger, but at the same time he respected her. She was the only one who could ever tell him what to do. He just built her a fantastic house."

* * *

The only thing resembling a decoration in Carlo's house is a large painting of a clown's face propped up against the wall. His face is made-up like a hobo, and he's wearing a dilapidated top hat. Large tears are rolling down his painted cheeks. The painting was Carlo's grandmother's and it's quite old, so he had it appraised.

"It isn't worth much," he said, "but I like it."

When he was a boy living in Boston, his father was in the Air Force.

"He divorced us when we were kids. I don't know where the hell he is now. I didn't get along with him, knocked about three of his teeth out, broke his jaw, put him in the hospital for six weeks one time. Because he divorced us when we were kids, never sent child support and all that bullshit... maybe that's another reason I don't want to get married, coming from a broken home. I don't really dwell on it, but somewhere in the back of my mind that might have something to do with it.

"When I was 21, he said 'If you guys have any bad feelings against me for leaving you when you were kids, we can step out back behind here and settle it'... meaning he wanted to fight. At the time I was into karate, kickboxing, which he didn't know. We walked out back, behind the pizza parlor we were at. He thought he was gonna kick my ass, so I front kicked him in the chest and I roundhouse kicked him in the face, and almost killed him. But I didn't have much regret about that because he was an asshole. My mother I like."

* * *

Only Floridians would venture into the searing 100 degree heat of a July afternoon to go fishing. Carlo met his friend Billy Katt at the boat ramp on the Loxahatchee River just north of Palm Beach. The heat didn't faze them, they were used to it. Their necks and shoulders were perpetually pink from the sun.

They launched Billy's old bass fishing boat quickly and dexterously. Billy backed the boat and trailer down the ramp, Carlo guided it into the water, and tied it up out of the way. Billy whipped the truck into the parking lot, and we were heading up river within minutes. Billy gunned her as fast as she'd go, making wide arcs and jumping back and forth in the wake of larger boats.

"So what else do you want to know about being single?" Carlo asked the author from New York who was covered from head to toe in Sunblock Number 29, holding on to the wobbly seat frame for dear life.

Carlo sat perched on the bow, enjoying the speed of the boat, trying to smoke a joint in the wind. Not one given to intro-spection, he said the pot helped him to think about things like where his life was and where it was going.

Billy suddenly slowed the boat down to a few miles an hour as the river narrowed and we came into the Jonathan Dickin-son State Park. Billy says he's cruised up this river nearly every weekend of his adult life and he never tires of the beauty of it. We were deep in the labyrinth of a mangrove swamp, islands of sand pine scrub and cabbage palms. The Cypress trees at this end of the river, where the water is brackish, are dead; twisted white skeletons of trees silhouetted against the deep blue of the sky. Ospreys build enormous nests in the uppermost joints of the dead branches.

It was quiet back there on the smooth, shallow water. We heard only the low buzz of the outboard motor and the cicadas' relentless hum. We watched for alligators. Carlo drew on his marijuana cigarette and got talkative.

"I don't chase women too much now. I'm different than I was a couple of years ago. Now, I work. I spend more time work-ing than anything else. I started my business five years ago part time. It's been up and down, just trying to teach myself. At night I have blueprints to look at. I have to worry about the next day's scheduling. Maybe it's better that way. I think, that way I'm not out on the streets.

"Sometimes I think relationships take so much of your time, whereas trying to start a business, or maintain a business takes a lot of time also, so fundamentally where I'm at is it's hard to have the both of them at the same time.

"I realize there's a lot of lonely people, everybody out there is looking for that special someone, but that's not where I'm at. I'm not that lonely, I don't mind being by myself. I like doing my work. That's what I enjoy. I'm not out there looking for a woman. Any relationship I get into now, the girl has to be willing to step back. Or else I just don't want to see her. It's that simple."

Billy is standing on the bow of the boat now, casting his fishing line 100 feet or so, then reeling it in, causing the silver and red lure to dance along the water. He's hoping to snag a tarpon or a bluefish.

"Carlo had a relationship once," Billy says. "Elaine. She was the most beautiful all-round person I've ever known. She was in high school with us, beautiful, but not one bit stuck up. The homecoming queen, Playboy centerfold material. Probably the only virgin in our high school, too. No one could figure it, but she lived with Carlo for about three years."

"Alright," says Carlo, "That was the one time I was in love and it didn't work and I thought in my heart that it would. While I was in love, I thought it would be forever. And when it wasn't forever... I fell head over heels in love, but then I fell out of love.

"Where do you go after that? Will I fall stronger in love with the next one? No, I don't believe that because I was too much in love. But all the pressures living with someone puts on you... I started looking at other women.

"I don't see myself falling in love again. Not the type of love I was in because it was too strong. And then to fall out of love... I don't trust myself. How am I supposed to know myself when I'm in love? How can I tell someone I'll love you forever, when I told someone else that and it didn't happen?"

"I remember the night you fell out of love with Elaine," Billy says. "It was about two in the morning and the phone rings and it's Carlo asking if he can sleep in my spare bedroom. So I say sure. And an hour later, he bangs on my door, wakes me up, and I open my door. Carlo has this girl in a full nelson, her t-shirt pulled up around her neck. 'You ever seen tits like this?'" he says to me. I could not believe it, the girl felt so ignorant.

"Elaine came banging on my front door later that night looking for Carlo. She was hysterical and I covered for him. Always regretted that. Elaine never forgave me."

Other boats drift past us occasionally, small motor boats and canoes rented from the State Park, commandeered by near-naked people shoring up their weekend tans, laughing as they try to master the art of paddling. One group has strapped together three or four canoes, the better to enjoy their floating party. Everyone, but everyone, has a beer can cocooned in a foam rubber holder to keep it cool. As we pass each craft, we study its inhabitants and they study ours, and we raise our beers in friendly salutes.

"I don't know," Carlo says, shaking his head. "You show affection to a woman, and they perceive it to be genuine, whether it is or not. Every woman wants to find a man to settle down with. I think their heads are floating. They want a man to love, who loves them, and everything's hunky dory. Well, I can be all hunky dory to them but for just one night. Then I don't see them anymore, because their attraction is stronger for me than mine is for them. So not to hurt them, or go any longer, I just stop seeing them before it goes anywhere."

* * *

We're far up river now, further than most of the canoes go. The water is fresh and the trees are dense. We're shaded by Australian Pines, Live Oaks and Cypress trees draped in Spanish moss. Billy points out a family of turtles sunning themselves on a half-submerged log. The banks of the islands are covered with ferns, cattail reeds, and bursts of white orchids.

What makes Carlo Morante tick? Can it be true that he doesn't need love and companionship? What does he need, want?

"Stability," he responds, "monetarily speaking. I'd like to be in a situation where I'm self-supporting, where I'd have enough rental units to where I wouldn't have to work if I didn't want to. I think what I do for a living is fun, I enjoy it, I like building. But I think I'd like to build without having to worry about any type of bills.

"It's not the bills so much, but just to feel that you've accomplished something. If you can reach a level that you feel satisfied that you've accomplished something in your life. Maybe you didn't reach your goal because your goal is too astronomical anyway. But at least you're stable. I feel if I owned 10 rental properties, and they're rented and paying for themselves, then I'd feel I had done something with myself that I could feel decent about myself with. Then I could start to relax.

"I think I may end up being a bachelor the rest of my life. I'm happy where I'm at right now. Let's put marriage in perspective where I'm at. One reason probably I didn't get married is it's like a trap. Once you're married, you're supposed to work hard, everything's set out for you what you're supposed to do. You're married, you're a couple, you vacation together, your whole life's laid out for you.

"Now a married man right now at my age with three or four kids, his ass had better be on the road if he ain't working, then looking for work. If he's not working and his wife is, he feels guilty. His wife is probably starting to nag him about getting work. I don't feel like getting henpecked. I'm down on bitching," he laughs.

"So at my age, 31, I have pressure from business but I don't have any of the total pressures of marriage. Single at 31 years, $240 a month mortgage, I can live in my house, it suits my purpose. The walls pouring out, right now I have other things I'm doing so this goes on the back burner. But do you think a woman could live in a house like mine? No, I would hear it every time I came in the door.

"No pressure on me. I come home. I sit down. I don't have somebody telling me what to eat, what time to be where, we made engagements for this or that. A lot of conflict, it's always a lot of conflict. I don't need it. Marriage is a big headache."

Waiting for Her

Billy Katt puts away his fishing rod and maneuvers the boat up a slender, twisted length of river. It's so narrow here, the trees' branches touch overhead, like fingers interlaced in prayer. Watching the mottled sunlight appear and disappear on the water's surface absorbs our attention, that and the sound of Carlo's resonant voice.

Billy is a person who's easy to be with because he's not uncomfortable with silence. You could know him 10 minutes and feel perfectly at ease sitting on a porch with him without talking. His evasion of chit chat is a relief. His stillness, like the river's, is soothing. Billy's been quietly listening to his friend's opinions, showing neither agreement nor surprise. He simply accepts Carlo, whom he's known since they were 15, even though they seem as different from each other as two men can be.

Whereas Carlo is dark, compact and solid, Billy is 6'3", long, thin and gangly. He has fair hair and the fair, easily sunburnt skin of his Irish genes. Carlo is intense and cocky; Billy is laid-back and soft-spoken, and has neither the looks nor the defiance necessary to be a lady killer. Carlo works for himself; Billy does framing and dry wall for general contractors. He's lived all his life in south Florida, not far from the Loxahatchee

River where he's gone fishing since he was a boy. He still goes, nearly every weekend. "Sometimes I don't even fish," he grins. "Just look at girls in bikinis."

At 31, he is like Carlo in one way. His days of trying to pick up girls at bars are, for the most part, behind him. In his 20s, that's what he did, but because he didn't have Carlo's natural talents, he met girls at bars by making them gifts of cocaine. And it worked: a few lines of cocaine in the bathroom or behind the building, and he'd have a girl's attention for the evening. Girls who got to know him grew to like him, and while he has many girls who are friends, it's been years since he's had a steady girlfriend until Janey.

Billy's dated Janey for the last eight months and he wants to marry her, but Janey has other plans. She's been married and divorced twice; she doesn't want to marry again, and she doesn't want children. Billy's set his mind on marrying her and having children.

"She's with her ex-husband today," Billy says dryly, as he turns the boat around to head back.

The bow runs aground near the bank and he uses an oar to release it from the gooey, black mud at the river's edge. The task accomplished, he lights a cigarette. He doesn't smoke much, but he virtually chain drinks cans of Miller Lite, which look tiny and insignificant encircled in his long fingers. He tilts his head back once, and down goes half a can of beer.

"It used to bother me that she sees him, but it doesn't much anymore," he continues. "They were married for 10 years, so I guess there's still something there. As long as she doesn't start seeing someone else, I can handle it. I don't like it, but I can handle it."

Down goes the other half of the beer, and he tosses the can

toward the stern where it lands with a dull clink on a pile of beer cans accruing in the hollow pit under the engine.

"She doesn't know what she wants, she really doesn't. I think she should see a therapist or something."

That's about enough talking for Billy in one day. When the river widens some, he asks Carlo to drive so that he can fish again. An hour later, we're back at the boat ramp, and they quickly load the boat back on the trailer. Carlo departs in his van, and Billy in his Chevy pick-up with a confederate flag for a front license plate.

It's a Saturday evening. Carlo may call up a woman he knows, if he feels like a woman's company, but it's more likely he'll work on his bookkeeping or study the blueprints of the house he's starting next week. He seldom listens to music or watches the old black and white television hooked to a VCR which he uses "only for pornos."

Billy returns to the house he owns with his mother in a small subdivision near Jupiter Beach. She's away for the weekend with her boyfriend. Everyone's away with some guy, he thinks. He kicks back in his E-Z boy recliner to watch reruns of his favorite sitcom, "The Addams Family." With a flick of a switch, he can bring Lurch, Uncle Fester, Thing and Morticia back to life for hours. Thank God for the VCR. His cat settles in his lap and he pops another Miller Lite. Very likely, he'll fall off to sleep in 10 minutes and won't wake up until it's time to go to bed.

Epilogue

Billy Katt did get married in 2000, but not to Janey. He remembers that "everything got easier" once he got married. He and his wife are devoted to one another and have only been separated twice in all these years: once for a wedding and once for a funeral.

Billy told us that Carlo Morante has "not changed one iota" in 25 years. Carlo never married. He runs a successful business and lives in a pricey condo on the Florida coast.

An Unwilling Bachelor

Maspeth, New York. A humble, working class neighborhood of row houses, asphalt playgrounds and grocery stores. Attached two-family dwellings with brick chimneys and neat, pitched roofs on shady streets. Welcome to Queens, a quick subway ride from Manhattan. Irish, Italian, Jewish families have been here since the term "melting pot" was invented. Too many cars, and not enough arteries.

Terry Wurth circles the track again and again. He slips into a smooth pace, completing his first mile in under six minutes. It's the middle of the day and the track is all his. He'll rest for five minutes before turning in another mile in under six. He'll alternate running and resting until he finishes his six-mile workout today.

On Saturday he finished first in the Master's Division of a five-kilometer race in Oyster Bay, Long Island. He outpaced fifty men in the over-forty class and finished eleventh in a field of three hundred men from the New York area. He's been a serious runner for ten years, ever since an ex-love of his told him, "You'll never be able to run."

"When I started running," he says, "I used her image and ran against it. I still do that, I still vent my anger and my rage in my running, and it works. When I run, I transcend my distress."

His running has progressed to where he's becoming a national contender. Plenty of rage to fuel that desire. To get into national contention, he has to get his five K time under eighteen minutes, and he's not far off.

"Victory is sweet," he says of Saturday's win. Even sweeter are the PRs, the personal records, he sets each time he goes out. A few months ago he joined the Withholds, an elite runners club for hardcore running addicts, known for its gut-breaking workouts. On Saturday when he felt like laying back, "I just told myself, 'I'm a Withhold runner now,' and got my second wind." Victory is sweet and "the high lasts almost indefinitely." He feels so good today that he trains harder than he might, pushing the envelope further and further back. When there isn't a woman in his life, he says, "I channel my libido into my running. Running can be really sexual," he says.

May loves watching Terry run. His German strength and Irish stoicism seem oddly lyrical, a fusing of Golden Gloves boxer, his working class upbringing and his training in sociology. May is thirty-eight and she finds the older man a refreshing change from most of the men she knows. But Terry is troubled about his experiences of late.

"I think I create a very masculine image, a very tough image which women like, but there is another part of me at this point in my life, I'm not into a power trip, I'm not into domination. I'm not into the kind of mental energy you need to plot, to control and so I'm somewhat laid back and when they realize this is the case, they're either disenchanted or they find this is an opportunity to be abusive to someone who ostensibly is strong.

"Maybe I appear to them to be more successful than I am even though I bend over backwards trying to play this down, I'm so aware of this; I try to present myself as honestly, as straightforwardly as possible, because if I create an illusion here, I'm going to get a disappointment reaction. Perhaps early on they look at me as more than I am. And it bothers the heck out of me that somehow I have to be so careful about how I present myself; it's really bothersome."

As Terry runs, May studies his physique. The longer he runs, the longer she can enjoy the sight of his strong legs pumping him into the distance, then charging him back on the other side of the track. She likes the way his tousled blond head grows smaller as he runs away, and larger as he runs back.

He runs another six-minute mile then rests; his next three miles leave him progressively shorter rest periods between faster runs. "When you push this hard, you're bound to have injuries," Terry says. A few years ago, he herniated his disk and it acts up from time to time. As he runs, he's aware of the pain.

May is aware that he was a heartthrob in his younger years. But at 52, Terry's in better shape than most men any age. He doesn't begin to look his age. There's a cockeyed boyish charm, a barely noticeable overbite that serves him well ("I don't know why, but women think it sexy"), and his hesitating speech, punctuated with bursts of eloquence and insight in the cadence of "Rocky Graciano does William Butler Yeats," is endearing to people who like him.

There's also the quiet confidence of a man who knows he can take care of himself; with his wiry quickness, he can make mincemeat of just about anyone in the ring, on the track, or on the slopes.

When he completes today's workout, he and May drive back to his house in Maspeth. He showers and finds May at the edge of the bed in a t-shirt. They make love constantly during the two months before the curtains come down.

* * *

Terry Wurth's Ph.D. in the sociology of sports took many years. He was already forty-eight when it came, twice married and divorced, with a love life more convoluted and longer than any quarter mile track. His catalogue of romantic experiences and wayward interludes is longer than his stride in the homestretch. But things got tougher as he got older.

"I have this feeling that you have a very competitive situation, particularly in the New York City area, you've got different age groups, and you've got socio-economic demographics, which define what is possible and what is not possible, what is likely and what is unlikely and the older you get, unless you're extremely wealthy or you have an extremely high status position you are likely to be more exposed to those people who are failing; and I have a further idea that what seems to happen is those people who have failed meet other people who are failing and the spiral of failure goes on... and I think people become so psychically damaged by this that at a certain point it's almost impossible to develop a lasting relationship."

Since the early eighties, Terry's lived off the small fortune he made when he sold his condo on West 4th Street. With the proceeds, he bought himself the life of Riley, summers at the beach, doing nothing but sunning, running and the ladies.

Ah, the ladies. There'd been a motley crew over the last six years, but more and more he kept running into the same type, the ones who serve the triumvirate god: "Success, Status, Power. More than any man, they want what a man brings," he says, "but the individual man, the man with all his faults, warts and frailties... not so much.

"The Christian virtues and character don't count with the new old maids. What counts is the superficiality. What counts is how many bucks you have, how much power you have, how important you appear to be. What happens is they're disappointed when I don't turn out to be as successful or as powerful as they initially perceive."

The Unwilling Bachelor and the New Old Maids: a love story for the eighties, taken from the Chronicles of the Unwed. The only thing harder for Terry right now than finding the right girl is finding the right job. He's an adjunct professor at a metropolitan university, which, roughly, means "part time," and part time isn't good enough anymore, in love or work.

"I could get consulting jobs doing sports research," he says, "but that's not going to be a full time job. I don't want that, I need to build up a pension plan, I need security, I need basic, long-term income so that's why I'm pursuing the academic career."

He presents the odd paper or two on the psychology of sports at a small college somewhere, and he's had schemes, like the one to establish a Boxing Foundation, but nothing's panned out just yet. So he runs, pushing for speed and miles, and when he wins, victory is sweet. But he's jobless and wifeless all the same.

Shy of moving to the plains of Winnipeg or the Dakotas, he'd go just about anywhere a teaching job came through. He wouldn't mind getting away from New York's social demographics anyway, away from the Bachelorettes.

* * *

He met Bachelorette #11 at a house party on Fire Island. She was aloof and snooty at first, but it progressed quickly, and over the last few months he'd been seeing her twice a week at her Upper West Side apartment. They got along fine for two months. Everything was swell until...

"I was floored when she started to criticize me for not being aggressive or assertive enough, like when a maître d' didn't move fast enough for her."

She was passionate, they had good sex together; she was athletic, they went on skiing holidays. He imagined staying with her a long, long time before she began to carp, before the picking turned vicious. He was surprised when it happened, but he knew it meant it wouldn't work out, it would be back to the drawing board again.

"I didn't think so at first. In the beginning she was loving and sweet, and I was hopeful, that here was a woman as good as she looks, who knew the facts of life." Who turned out to be just another Cosmopolitan Viper.

"May's career is her life, then some," Terry says. "She belongs to the Forum, the latest version of EST, works out at her health club two times a week, plays tennis, runs, skis a bit, has a high pressure, high visibility position with Goldman Sachs. Very funny woman, but overbearing after a while." She works late, and hard, and feels entitled to the best of everything. She comes from a brood of wealthy, high status lawyers and has been pushed since an early age to overachieve. Has a BA from here, an MA from there, that kind of thing.

Two months into his relationship with May, Terry began to notice the same cascading litany of objections and criticisms he'd encountered with other Bachelorettes.

He was sitting in front of his living room TV, loading up on his usual late-night dose of Cherry Garcia. Like he always did before trudging off to the bedroom to sleep. From the bedroom, through the closed door, May bitchily screamed, "Would you stop that damn slurping, Terry? I'm trying to sleep!"

He'd been extra quiet, he hadn't made a sound. The previous night, in her apartment on the Upper West Side, he wanted to watch a little TV after she went to bed, so he put on the earphones. With the earphones on, how could he disturb her? As he watched David Letterman he flipped absentmindedly through the pages of a magazine. May's eyes flashed open and she moaned, "You're making too much noise, Terry. I'm trying to sleep!"

Either she was an incredibly light sleeper, or she was a nut. He usually went to bed after her. One night he picked up a can of Raid in an attempt to spray a pesky moth into non-existence. May's familiar shriek startled him. She came into the doorway, and in a maniacally controlled voice she said, "You're really very inconsiderate, Terry. You can stay up and fuck around with that moth all night. Some of us have to be up in the morning, remember?"

She'd been digging him about his career. She didn't think he was ambitious enough. He wouldn't be a mere adjunct professor at 52 years of age if he'd applied himself. He was disorganized. She began to see that the scholarly jock was a wimp. The competitive runner was running away from instead of towards something.

May lit into him for tapping a pencil mindlessly on the table-top while she was writing checks. That night Terry sat dejectedly in bed watching TV with the sound off, just watching the flickering images on a screen.

She told him he was breathing too hard. Was he getting this straight? Maybe he shouldn't breathe at all, maybe that would make her High Holiness happy. The Princess snored lightly while she slept and frequently wakened in the middle of the night from bad dreams. In the morning she had awful breath; it could have peeled paint off a wall. But he didn't object, he didn't criticize her for not looking like a rose in the morning or not smelling as sweet. "You accept things about people, you go with the flow, you take the good with the bad, you make a relation-ship work." Didn't anyone have a concept of this anymore? If your relationship has a modicum of passion, respect, compati-bility, what more can you ask?

"Terry?"

"What now, my love? The sound is off."

"The damn flickering, it's keeping me up."

He flipped the remote and watched the TV subside into darkness. The room was dark, everything was still. A few minutes went by. He sat upright propped against the pillows and the headboard.

"Terry," she cried with more venom than before.

"Yes, darling?"

"I can't sleep if you're brooding in the dark." He could make out the sharp anger of her upper lip in a somnolent shadow of mounting rage.

"Sure, honey. Anything you say," came pleasant words laced with arsenic. What would it take to slip over the edge, to slip his hands around her pretty oh so pretty neck?

The Professor had no aptitude for practical things, not as measured by the Stockbroker. They'd go out to eat. She'd ask him what kind of food he was in the mood for and he'd say, "What-ever you like, I don't care."

"But what do you want?" she'd ask to no avail.

"Anything at all," he'd say. "I don't care."

"You must care, everyone cares," she'd whelp, but it was no use. It drove her nuts. It was symptomatic of his condition. He was a klutz, a gross incompetent who was going nowhere. What was she doing with him?

In the first two weeks of their relationship, she'd told a friend, "I've met the man I want to marry, I'm head over heels in love."

Her friend warned, "This time give it a chance, don't come down so hard on the guy. You know how you drive them away."

She'd held her tongue for two months. Now there was no way around the truth. He bugged her. She began to see him as part of the over-the-hill set. She couldn't imagine being with him the rest of her life. The boxer/professor was punch drunk. There were signs of mental/emotional dyslexia, lapses in memory, gaps in perception, an inability to tell left from right. Had early senility set in? Or had Emil Griffith simply clocked him one too many times?

* * *

For Terry, May's efficiency-of-movement theory was the proverbial last straw. She was so compulsive, so neurotic about it, and so hypercritical, that she brought the argument to his keys. His keys! It was a cold night and they were standing on the porch to his house. They'd just returned from a movie and he was having trouble locating his front door key. As she stood there waiting, she got more and more annoyed, then angrier and angrier.

She grabbed the keys out of his fumbling hands and announced, "Here, let me give you a basic lesson in efficiency. If you arrange your keys according to function," she said, as she shot the right key into the door and snapped open the latch, "you can do this with your eyes closed and maximize your time." She pushed into the vestibule in a huff and headed up the stairs. He watched her high-step it to the landing overhead.

"What if I don't want to maximize anything but the view?" he asked.

"Then you're going to find the view pretty boring, pretty fast."

"Ooh la la. Is that a threat?"

"You're a threat to yourself, Terry. You do everything haphazardly." She had his keys out on the kitchen table, she was removing them one by one and replacing them on the ring. As if she were talking to a little boy, not a man who had passed the half century mark, she instructed the Instructor, "It's really very simple, Terry."

Of course she had to be up early the next morning so he'd have to be quiet, nay, silent, when she went to sleep. He didn't want to be alone, but he didn't want to live like this. He couldn't even eat ice cream in front of the set like he used to. That was out now. Maybe he could read in the bathroom.

* * *

When he first met May, she warned him that she was "moody." He took that to mean "people say I'm not always happy" or that she sometimes felt depressed like anyone else. What he didn't know was that moody was a code word for abusive. He began to see that her passion for trivial criticism was a response to the overwhelming anxiety she felt about success, her fear that she wouldn't measure up, that she couldn't control the outcome, that she wouldn't get everything she was entitled to. She pressured him to conform to her.

"If I was Professor Emeritus, you'd find something else wrong with me," he lamented.

"At this rate you'll be Professor Emeritus by the turn of the century," she snapped back.

As she left the apartment for a power breakfast, the image of Terry sitting in his bathrobe at the kitchen table, tinkering with Mr. Coffee and leisurely reading the paper, stuck in her caw. She resented the latest disappointment in her dating career. Although he did give her the first screaming orgasm of her life. Of course her qualms about Terry hardly missed a beat, flooding back in as the orgasmic tide rolled back out.

Terry was disappointed too. Like other ambitious women he'd dated over the years, May didn't know when to stop. "I want it all and I'm gonna have it all!" she frequently blurted. Didn't she know that no one gets to have it all? That there is always a price to pay, and compromises? So now, instead of it all, she'd have Nothing Again. The relationship petered out. "We stopped seeing each other, except occasionally, to fuck," says Terry.

On her birthday he sent her a card: "Success. Power. Status. Three things I can't offer you on your birthday." May was offended. How barren the card was. He'd scribbled "May" at the top and "Terry" at the bottom and nothing more. She knew what he'd say, that it was a joke, but she knew it had been designed to provoke her.

* * *

Sitting in Sfuzzi's as he was doing this interview, a patron recognizes "Terrible Terry," as dubbed by *The New York Daily News* in 1956 during the Golden Gloves. "You fought Emile Griffith," says the fight freak, "in the Garden. You shoulda got the decision.

Over the years, Terry occasionally bumped into Emile Griffith and they talked about what would have happened if it had gone the other way. It wasn't one of the things Terry liked to dwell on. He exchanges a few fight memories with the stranger, then returns to the Bachelorettes.

"They're a phenomenon peculiar to large cities. They're attractive women, they have money, successful careers; they don't need men for financial support; they're usually in their thirties or forties; quite often they've never been married."

He is describing the very people surrounding us at Sfuzzi's, a place he selected for our meeting, where he seems likely to meet the women he complains about.

"There's something to that old canard about spinsters having a serious character flaw that keeps them alone all their lives. These sort of gals are cropping up all over the place. I think it's a function of age and multiple unsuccessful relationships, those are the key factors that add to this spiral."

Watching the dance of men and women getting as close to the bar as they can get, one wonders whether Terry expects to find love here, whether he expects to find love at all.

"No, no, no! I've become much more practical, pragmatic. I realize that those youthful fantasies or whatever they were don't exist any longer. I have no illusions, no. I do not want to grow old and be by myself.

"I feel that having someone is more important than being alone. I like the structure of having a woman, because when I don't have that what I tend to do is I seek — I seek all sorts of things. I seek sex, I seek companionship, I seek spontaneity; it's too haphazard for me so I really prefer a structure. And the structure I like most is with a woman."

These days, Terry's alone again. The only way out of the spiral of failure may be to change his demographics, move away from the new Amazons he feels are indigenous to large cities.

Most mornings, he sits at the kitchen table and drinks the freshly squeezed orange juice his mother usually prepares for him and leaves in his fridge. It's always tasty with just the right amount of pulp, just the way he likes it. His elderly parents rent him the top floor of their two-family house in Maspeth, on the block Terry grew up on as a kid. With his separate entrance and carport out back, he comes and goes as he likes.

After he eats, he drives to Victory Field on Woodhaven Boulevard for his daily workout. Racing for distance and speed. Pushing on, letting out. The angrier he gets, the closer he gets to an under eighteen five K race, and national contention.

"The speed workouts are the toughest, but they afford the greatest gains."

Too bad the same can't be said of relationships.

Epilogue

Terry Wurth found both the career and relationship he was struggling to find 26 years ago. At age 78, he's still pushing his physical limits. Today he's swimming not running, three miles an outing twice a week, turning in faster, cleaner laps than men half his age.

His academic career took off 15 years ago with articles he wrote on substance abuse and HIV and a book on the sports press and origins of baseball. Today the tenured associate professor of anthropology at a senior college within the City University of New York (CUNY) is not only on the verge of retirement, he's getting married. His fiancé Andrea is a vibrant 70 year-old who is the director of a contemporary art gallery. They've been together ten years. They plan to move to a home with a pool in Florida once they're wed.

VII. IMPERSONAL ADS

"Promise, large promise, is the soul of an advertisement."
Samuel Johnson

Mensa Gal's 'Scientific' Quest
for Perfect Mate

Katharine Estelle Steinberg, 36-year-old, Upper East Side New Yorker, isn't classically beautiful. Neither was Mata Hari; neither was Mae West, but they could make men believe they were just about the sexiest things alive. Estelle has the same gift. Her friends attest to the fact that she can target any man in any situation — bars, restaurants, bowling alleys, subway cars — and she can pick him up and take him home if she has a mind to. Estelle has chutzpa and she's funny. She can take control of nearly any situation, and seemingly any man. Yet in spite of the fact that she's gone out with hundreds of men, she has never found Mr. Right. She's never married.

Estelle is on the small side, with an average build, and a Mensa I.Q. Her most outstanding feature, other than her confidence, is the long, curly, auburn hair that she uses like a prop, constantly tossing it around to emphasize a dramatic point, or sweeping it all to one side with her perfectly manicured red-tipped fingernails.

She grew up in a well-to-do, Jewish family on Long Island, the middle daughter of three. Something in the mix of heredity and environment produced Estelle: one part Jewish American

Princess, one part good ol' broad. Her cultured upbringing and fluent French steered her into her career as a Socialite Worker, requiring no M.S.W. and paying a lot better. She's traveled the world as the personal assistant to rich and powerful people. Her friends call her "the handmaiden to the stars." Estelle works as little as possible, and has been known to take long vacations, i.e., a year or two, between jobs.

She's always had a preference for younger men. As she puts it, "I was famous for younger boys before Cher was born. I like them, they're amusing."

At the urging of her mother and her friends, Estelle has decided to try to meet some 'older men.'

"Try someone who's 40," her mother said. "Someone old enough to put up with you."

Estelle thought she would go about her search for the perfect mate scientifically. She turned to the Personal Ads in *New York Magazine*, figuring it was easy, safe, and she didn't have to leave her apartment to do it. She wrote amusing, pithy responses to several ads that she guessed were placed by older men.

"At first I'm reading these ads thinking these people are all definitely massive losers, I'm positive. They go right from Singles Night at the Y to placing *New York Magazine* ads. Wait a minute Estelle, I say to myself, it's conceivable that you might place an ad, and you're not a loser are you? And I'm like, no you're not. You sure? No, you're not. OK, just checking. So, give these people a chance. All right, fine."

One ad Estelle answered turned out to be from Irwin. It read:

> *What Does A Man Have To Do To find love, dating and possible marriage in this crazy world? I hate eating, sleeping and traveling alone. Good looking,*

single, Jewish, witty male, 45, all alone, athletic,
professional, independent business owner. House
in Southampton. 5'10", trim, enjoy baseball, books,
movies, dancing, shows. Seeking an attractive lady
who is classy, warm and a good conversational-
ist and who can laugh. Note/phone/photo. Take a
chance in life. I did.

Estelle sent her reply to the listed box number on a Monday.
On Thursday, she answered her phone and was greeted with
a loud, nasal man's voice with a heavy Bronx accent crying
"KATHY!"

(My name is Katherine Estelle. You can call me any combination... you can call me Katherine, you can call me Estelle. But
Kathy is not my name and I get shivers up my spine.)

KATHY... THIS IS IRWIN. (He's screaming. I didn't even
need a phone to hear him.) YOU ANSWERED MY AD IN
NEW YORK MAGAZINE. I LIVE IN RIVERDALE. DO YOU
KNOW WHERE THAT IS?

Uh-huh.

WHERE?

What is this, Double Jeopardy?

I'M ASKING. I'M JUST ASKING.

Upper Bronx, almost Westchester but not quite.

YOU KNOW IT! YOU KNOW IT!

(I'm scoring big points already. I know where Riverdale is.)

SO WHAT DO YOU LOOK LIKE?

I'm gorgeous.

YOU KNOW... I GOT A LITTLE HEAVY, BUT YOU
KNOW I'M LOSING THE WEIGHT. I GO OUT, I HAVE
A NICE PIECE OF FISH, STEAMED VEGATABLES. YOU

KNOW, YOU GET A LITTLE MIDDLE THERE.

(I'm like is this fascinating or what? I cannot cope. I don't care if he's the nicest guy in the world with his house in Southampton, I can't stand the sound of his fuckin' voice. The thought of that voice, waking me up in the morning. KATHY, CAN I GET YOU COFFEE? YOU KNOW WHAT COFFEE IS? YOU KNOW WHERE IT COMES FROM? I'm going mental from this guy. I try to be nice to him. I take deep breaths and say:)

Listen I'm going out for dinner. Why don't you give me your number, I'll give you a buzz...

WELL, TELL ME WHEN YOU'RE COMING BACK, I'LL CALL YOU.

Irwin, I'll be back when I'm done eating.

WELL, WHAT TIME IS THAT?

Well, that depends if I chew quickly or slowly.

I'LL CALL YOU BACK.

Irwin called Estelle back as promised and left this message on her answering machine:

KATHY, IT'S IRWIN. I'M CALLING YOU BACK. YOU'RE NOT HOME. YOU MUST BE HAVING DINNER. YOU'LL GIVE ME A BUZZ OR I'LL CALL YOU.

Another message was recorded on her answering machine.

KATHY, IT'S IRWIN. I DON'T UNDERSTAND. YOU'RE NOT ANSWERING MY CALLS. YOU WROTE ME A NICE LETTER, KATHY. I LIKED YOUR LETTER. YOU WROTE TO ME. I DON'T GET THIS. I THOUGHT WE COULD GO OUT.

"Fuckin' nightmare from hell, Irwin and the nice piece of fish. I wished salmonella on him. That was Irwin."

Then there was Barry:

Good Looking and Desirable Jewish male, 38, who is in control of his life is searching for a beautiful and intelligent lady, so that we both may enjoy theater, dining, romantic evenings, sports, laughs, good conversation. Photo.

Barry called Estelle and they made tentative plans to go out on Saturday night. When he learned she once worked for a financial services company, he wanted to bring the video of "Wall Street" to Estelle's apartment to watch on the VCR. She nixed that, but said they could meet somewhere else, on neutral ground.

"So Barry was gonna go out with me Saturday night. This was on Tuesday I talked to him. Then he never calls back, but I don't give a damn. The next week, on Thursday he leaves a message on my machine. His voice is irate, frantic. He says, 'Estelle! This is Barry. Where *are* you? I'm in your neighborhood and I thought I was gonna come over??!!'

"We'd never made plans for Thursday. In my mind, he'd stood me up for Saturday, not that it mattered. He doesn't even know me, and he's irate that he's around the corner and I'm not there waiting for him! Right, this guy is really 'in control of his life.' So much for Barry."

Next!

Trial Date — Jewish attorney, wears power tie, 5'11", handsome. Wants to tie the knot with a not-high-powered career or just plain gal. Brief letter/photo.

"The Jewish attorney calls me up. He lives in New Jersey. He says, I should come for the weekend. I said whoa, whoa, what's the matter with coffee? Haven't you heard of a drink? I should come for the weekend? What if I hate you, what if you want to slit my throat? He had a boarding house for college girls. Interesting. Another weirdo.

Estelle knew she was really jumping into it when she answered this ad:

> *Want to Have a Child? An unusual bachelor with paternal instincts, not ready to get married for philosophical reasons. Jewish, 36, very good looking, healthy and smart. Looking for a strong, special woman with similar qualities for a relationship and a lifetime commitment to our child.*

His name turned out to be Alex and he was from Sweden. He liked Estelle over the phone and wanted to meet her.

"But he was weird. He would call me, I wouldn't be home, I'd leave a message on his machine. One day he calls me up and blasts me. 'Estelle! This is Alex. (He's shouting in a thick Swedish accent.) I thought you'd call me back, and you never called me back! And then you called me back, and I didn't realize that the message that you called back was a new message! It sounded like an old message you left me, and I didn't realize. But after your message, there were two other messages, which were after the time of your first message, so I knew it had to be a second message, and that you did call me back. And now I'm calling you back.'

"I had to take a valium to listen to my machine at that point." So much for Alex.

Oh, yes, how could she forget Jay:

Creative Professional Man, 39, attractive, fit and successful. Seeking intelligent, successful, pretty lady, 40, to share friendship, fun and romance.

"Jay, I call him Gay Jay. Jay sounded gayer than the 4th of July. He left a message on my machine, 'Estelle, this is Jay. I'm at SEVEN... ONE... EIGHT.' (I felt like it was a telethon and he's holding up the numbers.) 'Estelle, when you call me back, please be sure to call only between 7:15 and 9 in the evening.' (What, his wife doesn't want to be disturbed when she's reading the kids a bedtime story?)

Turns out Jay owns a personnel agency. He sends the workers home at 7:15 and he stays till 9. Because he doesn't let the workers take personal calls, he has to set a good example. Estelle calls him back at 8 p.m. as instructed.

"I take a class at Hunter College on Friday nights," he says. "We could meet for coffee for about five minutes before my class."

"Right Jay, why don't we just meet at the drive-through at McDonalds?"

"Oh, is there a McDonald's up there?"

"Sorry Jay. I only have two minutes. I can't give you the full five. So I can't make it on Friday night between 6:30 and 6:35."

Naturally, she blew him off.

Several months later, Jay called Estelle back.

"This is Jay, we had spoken a while ago. I don't know if you remember me... ."

(How could I forget him? He sounds like a fuckin' Rockette!)

"So why are you calling me back, Jay? Didn't you have any success with your ad? Did you meet anyone wonderful?"

"Well, I met one person."

"What happened to her?"

"She moved to Florida."

(Probably after a date with you, Australia was too close!)

"Listen," he says, "we could meet for 15 minutes a week from Friday." (15 minutes! He must be desperate now.) "This weekend I'll be in Florida."

"Oh yeah, give me a buzz when you get back. I'd love to get together." (Just not with you, Gay Jay.)

* * *

Out of the all the *New York Magazine* ad men who called Estelle, she did not agree to meet a single one. She thinks her original theory was right: they are all "massive losers." Back to the drawing board, Estelle. Is she getting discouraged? Does she still hope to meet Mr. Right?

"It depends... some days I do, sometimes I don't. Some days I'm happy to be home reading a book. Other days, it's like someone's gotta be out there. You go through these head trips where you think, am I the worst person in the world, the ugliest person, the fattest, the least intelligent? Here are people four times my size, one quarter my IQ, walking around with a husband and children. So it's like... go figure. Who knows? And who knows what their life is really about?"

What about the so-called primal need to bond, Estelle?
"No problem," she quips, "I get my bonding from the dentist."

Epilogue

Sorry, there isn't one. Estelle, if you're out there and read this, let us know at www.Single-in-America.com.

www.ingramcontent.com/pod-product-compliance
Lightning Source LLC
Chambersburg PA
CBHW032110280326
41933CB00009B/778